The Raven

Rio Nuevo Publishers®
P.O. Box 5250, Tucson, Arizona 85703-0250
(520) 623-9558, www.rionuevo.com

See page 117 for photography and illustration credits.

Library of Congress Cataloging-in-Publication Data

Hassler, Lynn.
The Raven : soaring through history, legend & lore / Lynn Hassler.
    p. cm.
ISBN 978-1-933855-13-4
1. Ravens. 2. Ravens—Folklore. I. Title.
QL696.P2367H36 2008
 598.8'64—dc22

                                    2007023218

Design: Karen Schober, Seattle, Washington.

Printed in Canada.

10 9 8 7 6 5 4 3 2 1

THE
Raven
SOARING THROUGH HISTORY,

LEGEND & LORE

LYNN HASSLER

RIO NUEVO PUBLISHERS

TUCSON, ARIZONA

Contents

Introduction

These are what my father calls
our raven days. The phrase is new
to me. I'm not sure what it means.
If it means we're hungry, it's right.
If it means we live on carrion,
it's right. It's also true
that every time we raise a voice
to sing, we make a caw and screech,
a raucous keening for the dead,
of whom we have more than our share.
But the raven's an ambiguous bird.
He forebodes death, and yet he fed
Elijah in the wilderness
and doing so fed all of us.
He knows his way around a desert
and a corpse, and these are useful skills.

—FROM "RAVEN DAYS," BY ANDREW HUDGINS,
in *BIRDS IN THE HAND: FICTION AND POETRY ABOUT BIRDS*, 2004

A SINGLE LARGE BIRD CLOAKED IN BLACK UTTERS A LONG-drawn-out *croak* as it sails through the air, long pointed wings set against the vast blue sky. With relaxed, languid wing beats, it moves rapidly through the air, then climbs upward, wheels and turns, and suddenly tumbles downward in an impressive dive. This aerodynamically sleek, pitch-black bird is the Common Raven, one of the most widespread wild birds in the world. Highly developed animals with an impressive array of vocalizations, Common Ravens are the largest members of the corvid, or crow, family, and the largest bodied of all of the passerine, or perching, birds.

Found in both the Old and New Worlds, Common Ravens are distributed throughout major portions of North America, Europe, Asia, and North Africa. This versatile, cosmopolitan creature is able to live successfully in many diverse habitats: on ice floes, in the Arctic tundra, in grasslands, deserts, and mountains, and along rocky cliffs and seacoasts. It is equally at home in large urban areas.

Because of its ability to thrive in so many different environments, some Native American tribes regard the raven as the most powerful of all birds. Other kinds of birds are simply not adaptable or clever enough to live in the coldest and hottest places on earth, as well as in the largest, most polluted cities of the world.

Other indigenous peoples say that the raven is so powerful and mighty because it was the actual creator of the world, or at least played a significant part in the process. Some believe that it created man, but whether humans actually came out of a clamshell or a pea pod is anybody's guess. Some cultures have associated ravens with darkness and death, healing and magic. In Europe, ravens were seen feeding on carrion from battlefields and attacking crops, and were regarded as destructive creatures. Some believe the bird is a messenger between the living and spiritual worlds, with the ability to bring back the souls of the dead.

Throughout time these ebony-hued birds have served as inspiration for legends, literature, art, vocabulary, religion, and music, and it is no exaggeration to say that they have influenced human civilizations throughout the world. Thought to be incredibly wise by some cultures, ravens are considered to be silly and flighty by others. Part of their mystique comes from humanlike personalities, which show rather opposing characteristics: at times they have been perceived as good, other times as evil. They've been associated with death but also with good fortune. Are these birds earthly or spiritual? Rebels or lawmakers? Hoodlums or do-gooders? Because of their twofold characters, ravens have been regarded both with awe and terror, suspicion and respect. Whatever one's take on these majestic, obsidian-colored birds, one thing is certain: these are creatures to be noticed and reckoned with.

THEIR INCLUSION IN LITERATURE IS EXTENSIVE, from the Bible to modern-day fables. Likewise, the influence of corvids on language is significant—think "crowbar," "scarecrow," "crow's feet," "ravenous," "raving maniac," and "rave up." Let's look at some of the words we often associate with these birds, noting their proximity to our feathered friend's own entry in the *American Heritage Dictionary.*

RAVEN: *n.* a large bird having black plumage and a croaking
cry. *adj.* black and shiny. *v.* to consume greedily, devour or
to seek or seize as prey or plunder; to eat ravenously

RAVENOUS: extremely hungry, voracious, predatory

RAVENING: greedily predacious

RAVING MANIAC: behaving irrationally

RAVE UP: a raucous party, a wild or vigorous musical performance

In the British Isles the countryside is littered with place names reflecting a corvid history: Ravenglass, Raven Beck, Ravensnest Wood, Ravens Close. In Scotland ravens are referred to as corbies; hence there is a Corb Glen, Corbie Head, and Corbys Crag. In North America there is Ravenswood, West Virginia; Raven Creek, Pennsylvania; Ravensworth, Virginia; the Raven Fork Stream in the Great Smoky Mountains National Park; and the village of Ravena, New York, where "friendly spirits pervade."

If you search the Internet for "raven," you'll get matches for everything from Native American fetishes, totem poles, and masks, to references in literature and poetry, to athletic team mascots and rock bands. Raven school mascots generally sport large heads, reflecting the notion that these birds have exceptional memory and great intelligence, obviously a plus on the playing field. If you're a football fan, perhaps you root for the NFL Baltimore Ravens. If you're a coffee aficionado, maybe you've enjoyed a cup of the steamy stuff from Raven's Brew Coffee in Ketchikan, Alaska, where the slogan is "The Last Legal High." Or maybe you've sipped a glass of zinfandel from California-based Ravenswood

"Raven" in Languages around the World

A University of Georgia anthropologist has confirmed approximately 181 names for crows and ravens; this is from 136 different human languages on at least five separate continents. Many of these words are onomatopoetic; that is, the word is similar to the cry or call of the bird. Please note that as language continues to evolve and adapt, spellings may vary.

Cherokee	Kalanu	Latin	Corvus
Cree	Kahka'kwi	Navajo	Gáagii
Danish	Ravn	Old English	Hr fn, Hremm, Hremn
Dutch	Raaf	Polish	Kruk
Esperanto	Korvo	Portuguese	Corvo
Finnish	Korppi	Russian	Bópoh
French	Corbeau	Sanskrit	Kaaka, Kârava
Gaelic	Bran	Scots Gaelic	Fitheach, Fhitich
German	Rabe	Slovenian	Krókar
Greek	Korax	Spanish	Cuervo
Hopi	Adoko	Swedish	Korp
Hungarian	Holló	Turkish	Kuzgun
Icelandic	Hrafn	Ukrainian	Bópoh
Inuit	Tulugaq	Vietnamese	Dahn tù
Irish	Fiach	Welsh	Cigfran
Italian	Corvo	Yiddish	Woron
Japanese	Karasu	Yup'ik	Tulukaraҟ
Lakota	Kangi'	Zuni	Kotollo-ah

Winery. Its logo shows three intertwined ravens with the byline: "No wimpy wines."

There's a Ravens' Cycle Racing Team in Dublin, Ireland, that hopes to win competitions with the speedy, skillful raven behind it, and a friendly neighborhood pub in North Vancouver, British Columbia, is dubbed The Raven. Buddy Holly wrote a tune called "Raven On," and on the Emmy award–winning sitcom series on the Disney Channel called *That's So Raven,* the main character (Raven Baxter) uses psychic skills and powers of disguise to get herself, her family, and her friends out of trouble. The show's theme song has a refrain that goes: "That's So Raven./It's a Future I can see./That's So Raven./It's so mysterious to me."

At the University of Virginia there is an old and very prestigious group of scholars called the Raven Society, named in honor of the illustrious poem "The Raven," written by that university's most celebrated alumnus, Edgar Allan Poe. In Munich, Germany, lives the International Youth Library (IYL), home of the largest book collection of international children's literature in the world. Language specialists there select newly published books that they consider to be noteworthy and give them the "White Raven" accolade, testimony to the impressive character of these birds.

The Raven's Eye is an aboriginal newspaper published in the Yukon and British Columbia. The Yukon takes raven worship one step further: in June 1985, the Yukon Territory passed the Raven Act, designating it as the official territory bird. In Lithuania there's a Young Raven beer, reportedly developed to accompany the national dish of crow. Ravens are portrayed on postage stamps in

Similarities between Ravens and Humans

- Most human beings manage the business of life during the daytime. Ravens are also diurnal, hunting for food and water, courting, mating, and building nests during daylight hours.
- Ravens rely on vision to search for food and to locate and avoid danger. Humans also depend upon visual clues for their daily existence.
- Humans enjoy talking and communicating; ravens are loquacious as well.
- Ravens are companionable, and humans tend to flock together. Human beings tend to live in family units, as do ravens.
- Ravens use memory for retaining images and locations of food sources. Humans rely on retaining and recalling past experiences as they move forward in life.
- Human beings are generalists in terms of the foods they consume, dining on a myriad of meats, vegetables, fruits, and grains. Ravens are omnivorous and are equally diversified when it comes to eating.
- Ravens are relatively long-lived when compared to other members of the passerine order. The record life span for a banded wild raven is thirteen years; some ravens in captivity have lived for more than forty-four years. And, of course, human beings live longer than any other primate species.

many different countries, from Bhutan to Finland, from Turkmenistan to the United States.

While they are popular and revered by many people, crows and ravens are considered by some to have a few downsides. Fear of these mysterious birds, something we call corvophobia, generally exists among people who have watched Alfred Hitchcock's 1963 horror movie *The Birds* one too many times. Some object to the fact that these black bandits steal the eggs of our cherished songbirds—but hey, ravens have to eat too. Farmers resent them because they may feed on crops in agricultural fields; but the number of agricultural pests that they consume far offsets any damage inflicted. Ranchers often look unfavorably upon ravens because they harass livestock and reportedly pluck the eyes of newborn lambs—survival of the fittest? And then there is that disgusting habit of feeding on rotting carcasses. But isn't that nature's way of cleaning up?

Let's face it: ravens are everywhere, and continue to pervade our cultures. They are brash, mysterious, playful, mischievous, acrobatic, intelligent, and downright intriguing. How can we not admire them?

The Corvid Family

On a withered branch
a crow has settled—
autumn nightfall

—BASHŌ, TRANSLATION BY
HAROLD G. HENDERSON, 1958

ON A CLEAR NIGHT IN SPRING, you might be able to find a
group of stars called Corvus (the Crow), a small but glittering constellation of the southern skies. The complete shape of a sitting crow
is visible only under the best of conditions, but the four brightest
stars of the cluster form a quadrangle and may be readily spotted.
How this constellation came to be is part of Greek mythology:

A raven (or perhaps a crow) served the god Apollo and was sent
forth to fetch water. On its journey it spied a fig tree located next to
a pond. The raven decided to wait until the figs ripened and then

he slowly ate scads of the tasty fruits. He then spotted a water snake and decided to use the serpent as an excuse for his tardiness in returning to his master. After finally obtaining water in a cup, he took it and the snake back to Apollo. According to legend, Apollo saw through this fraud and in his anger cast the bird, the cup, and the snake into the skies, where they became three constellations—the Crow (Corvus), the Cup (Crater), and the Serpent (Hydra).

The Corvidae are a diverse group of passerine, or perching, birds. Wherever you live, you've probably seen at least one member of this family. Noticeable because of their brash ways, strident calls, and unmelodious voices, this diverse assemblage includes the all-black crows and ravens, as well as jackdaws, jays, magpies, nutcrackers, and the rook.

Although dulcet tones may not be their strong point, corvids are thought to be uncommonly intelligent. Versatile, adaptable, omnivorous, and opportunistic, they are able to live successfully in many different habitats. As a group, they are known for their habit of hiding surplus food to retrieve at a later time.

Members of the crow family are also renowned for their thieving ways. For example, there is a Swedish expression, "steal like a raven." Ravens pirate eggs and food from other birds. They will sometimes sneak up behind nesting hawks, eagles, or turkey vultures and pull on their tail feathers; then when the nesting birds are distracted and away from their nests, other ravens swoop in to nab the prized eggs. Ravens routinely raid seabird colonies, gormandizing on both eggs and nestlings. Thugs? I don't think so. Opportunists? Yes, most definitely.

Ravens of the World

Some researchers speculate that corvids originated from an Australian ancestor that "escaped" to Asia about twenty to thirty million years ago. Since that time, the adept raven has discovered many suitable climates and environments.

SCIENTIFIC NAME	COMMON NAME	RANGE
Corvus cryptoleucus	Chihuahuan Raven	Arid southwestern United States to central Mexico
Corvus coronoides	Australian Raven	Southern and eastern Australia
Corvus mellori	Little Raven	Southeastern Australia
Corvus tasmanicus	Forest Raven	Tasmania and adjacent southern coast of Australia
Corvus ruficollis	Brown-necked Raven	Cape Verde Archipelago; north Africa to west Pakistan
Corvus rhipidurus	Fan-tailed Raven	Sub-Saharan Africa, southern Middle East, and Arabian Peninsula
Corvus albicollis	White-necked Raven	East and southeast Africa
Corvus crassirostris	Thick-billed Raven	Ethiopia and Eritrea
Corvus corax	Common Raven	Arctic regions, Asia, middle Europe, North America, and Central America

Let's return to the constellation Corvus, where the notion of thievery is once again evident. Located beneath the Virgin's head in the Virgo complex, the bill of the raven/crow points toward Spica, the jewel of the Virgin, as if waiting for just the right opportunity to seize this gem.

Birds in the crow family tend to be stocky in appearance, with heavy bills. While they vary in size and color, all have strong legs and feet, grasping toes, and stout, heavy bills. Most members of the group, including ravens and crows, have stiff rictal bristles (modified feathers), which help to protect their nostrils. The nostrils, or external nares, are the beginning of the air passages and allow birds to breathe without opening their mouths.

Some members of the corvid family nest in loose colonies. Various species of jays practice cooperative breeding, in which several adults tend the young in the nest. Most corvids, however, nest in isolated pairs. Many forage for food mainly on the ground, but also in trees. Some members of the family hop while on the ground, while others walk almost exclusively.

Many of the corvids are primarily black or blue in color, although some are boldly patterned with bright colors. The dazzling Green Jay, found from subtropical south Texas to Venezuela and northern Bolivia, is painted in shades of emerald, yellow, and cobalt blue.

While there are many different species of ravens and crows throughout the world, the largest member of the family, and certainly the most cosmopolitan, is the Common Raven, *Corvus corax*. *Corvus* is Latin for "raven" or "crow." The species name *corax* is from the Greek *korax,* meaning a "croaker," a reference to the raven's guttural call. The common name "raven" is from an old Norse word *hrafn,* meaning "to clear one's throat."

Ravens and Crows

The terms "raven" and "crow" are often used interchangeably in legend and lore. Some people regard ravens as oversized crows, while others regard crows as raven "wanna-bes." There are Hooded Crows, Fish Crows, Carrion Crows, Cape Crows, House Crows, and many others living throughout the world. Likewise, there are many species of ravens: Forest Raven, Chihuahuan Raven, Fantailed Raven, and Australian Raven, to name a few. In North America, the two most widespread and common species are Common Raven (*Corvus corax*) and the American Crow (*Corvus brachyrhynchos*). While these two birds look remarkably alike and have similar behavioral traits, it is possible to tell them apart.

Ravens are the larger of the two species and weigh about three times more than the average crow—the latter a lightweight at less than a pound. Ravens sport prominent, heavy beaks with a curved culmen, or ridge, on top; the crow's bill is less bulky looking. Raven wings are narrower and extend to some 4–4½ feet; the crow's wingspan is about 3 feet. Size is always difficult to judge in the field, but the shape of the tail also separates the two: the raven's is longish and wedge-shaped, the crow's short and rounded. In flight, ravens alternate between flapping and sailing—gliding on flat wings. Crows tend to glide, holding their broad wings in a

The Classification of Ravens and Crows

To make sense of the great diversity of nature, scientists classify living things into organisms. Taxonomy is the scientific discipline of naming organisms on the basis of their supposed evolutionary relationships. It is important to note that scientific classification is constantly changing, and that experts continue to debate about how the categories (genus, species, etc.) are defined. Here is an overview of how ravens and crows fit into the natural order:

Kingdom: Animalia

Phylum: Chordata (includes all vertebrates and a few invertebrates)

Class: Aves (birds)

Order: Passeriformes (perching birds, also called passerines)

Family: Corvidae (the corvid or crow family—includes ravens, crows, jays, magpies, nutcrackers, jackdaws, choughs, treepies, and the rook; more than 100 species worldwide)

Genus: Corvus (worldwide includes ravens, crows, jackdaws, and the rook)

Species: worldwide, 9 species of ravens, 31 species of crows, 1 rook, and 2 jackdaws

slight upward dihedral or V-shape. Their wing tips are more rounded than the pointy wing tips of the Common Raven.

Elongated feathers on the raven's throat, known as hackles, give the birds a rather uncombed, shaggy appearance. Crows, on the other hand, lacking significant hackles, look smooth and tidy.

Males and females are identical in appearance in both species, although males are sometimes slightly larger. Both ravens and crows have varied voices, but the ravens' calls tend to be quite guttural. The higher-pitched caw of a crow seems almost feeble compared to the hoarse, resonant croak of the raven. Crows often congregate in large assemblages, while ravens are less gregarious, often traveling alone, or are seen in pairs or in small groups. A group of crows is called a "murder," a flock of ravens a "terror" or an "unkindness"—rather uncomplimentary terms for these intriguing creatures.

In addition to physical characteristics, humans have also noted differences in the behavior of the raven and the crow. From naturalist and author Barry Lopez comes this distinction, found in *Desert Notes: Reflections in the Eye of a Raven*:

> One morning four ravens sat at the edge of the desert
> waiting for the sun to rise. They had been there all night
> and the dew was like beads of quicksilver on their wings.
> Their eyes were closed and they were as still as the cracks in
> the desert floor.
>
> The wind came off the snow-capped peaks to the north
> and ruffled their breath feathers. Their talons arched in the
> white earth and they smoothed their wings with sleek, dark
> bills. At first light their bodies swelled and their eyes flashed
> purple. When the dew dried on their wings they lifted off
> from the desert floor and flew away in four directions.
> Crows would never have had the patience for this.

These distinctions pass from science to legend. Aesop's fable called "The Crow and the Raven" alludes to the differing status of the two: The raven was greatly respected by mankind as a fortune-teller, and this made the crow green with envy. One day the crow spotted some wayfarers along the road and decided this would be a good opportunity to assert itself. From the branches of a tree, it began to caw loudly. The travelers were alarmed at the shrill cawing, fearing that it might portend misfortune for them. However, when they looked carefully at the bird they sighed with relief because it was not a raven at all. It was a crow, a bird of little import that had no power to foretell the future.

Brainy Birds

Tha gliocas an ceann an fhitich,
meaning, "There is wisdom in a raven's head."

—Scots Gaelic proverb

In Ireland, the phrase "raven's knowledge" means to see and to know all. It has long been recognized that members of the corvid family display exceptional intelligence and instinct, two characteristics that have earned them respect throughout history. An aptitude for taking advantage of new and ever-changing situations, coupled with a knack for exploiting the activities of human beings for their own benefit, certainly gives the impression that these are intelligent creatures.

The Roman naturalist Pliny the Elder was one of the first to relate a story of a raven exhibiting great acumen. Whether it was a raven or a crow is unclear, but the gist of the story is as follows:

During a time of drought, a raven found a bucket of water and needed to raise the liquid so that it would be high enough for it to drink. To complete this task, the bird proceeded to drop a number of rocks or stones into the bucket, successfully raising the water level. An Aesop tale titled "The Crow and the Pitcher" tells this same story, concluding with the moral: "Necessity is the mother of invention."

One of America's first ornithologists, U.S. Army Major Charles Bendire, had a pet crow named Jim that he often teased with a knife, keeping the sharp implement just out of the bird's reach. One day while playing this game, instead of nipping at the glistening blade, Jim figured out that if he bit at the major's hand, it would cause him to drop the knife. And so he did. Legend has it that the crow dropped down, picked up the knife, flew off with it, and stashed it away, never to be seen again.

Ravens exhibit great cleverness, especially when it comes to eating. In northerly climates, they have been known to tug on fishing lines left unattended by ice fishermen. This requires a certain amount of perception—to pull on a string without actually seeing the reward (a fish) at the end. They must secure the string with their strong feet, then pull it up, and repeat this process until the end (and hopefully the fish) is above the ice and within reach.

In another observation of ingenious innovation, Victorian ornithologist R. Bosworth Smith noted in his 1905 title, *Bird Life and Bird Lore*:

> Another Raven, kept in a yard, in which a big
> basket sparrow-trap was sometimes set,

watched narrowly the process from his
favourite corner, and managed, when the trap
fell, to lift it up, hoping to get at the sparrows
within. They, of course, escaped before he
could drop the trap. But, taught by experience,
he opened communications with another tame
Raven in an adjoining yard, and the next time
the trap fell, while one of them lifted it up, the
other pounced upon the quarry.

The ravens' capability of visualizing a distant reward shows impressive mental acuity. The clever birds have also been noted gathering bread, crackers, and other dry food items and ferrying them to a wet puddle or pool for a good soaking—a way of softening up the entrée before dining. Some observers have seen ravens collecting crackers left by picnickers and stacking them up in a pile. Obviously it is more efficient to move an entire pile in one fell swoop rather than one cracker at a time, and this is exactly what the ravens did.

Candace Savage's 1995 book, *Bird Brains,* describes how German ethologist Otto Koehler had an inkling that ravens had an innate instinct about numbers and that they might even be able to count. Otto just happened to own a raven named Jacob that lived in his laboratory. With Jacob as his lab "rat," he designed a series of experiments to test out his theory. Koehler deposited a set of small boxes before the bird. The boxes were distinguished with marks numbering two through six. In addition to the boxes, small objects in groups of two, three, four, five, and six were placed before Jacob. These objects and boxes were all different in both size and shape, and their lineup changed during each test. Jacob simply needed to match the correct box with the correct number of objects. If he achieved this goal, there was a reward—food, of course. Apparently Jacob was consistently successful, indicating to Koehler that his pet was capable of counting to six.

Zoologist and animal behaviorist Bernd Heinrich, who has studied ravens extensively, credits these birds with being "the brains of the bird world." Nobel Prize winner Konrad Lorenz also credits ravens with the highest mental development of all birds, rivaled only by mynas and parrots. Apparently parrots and corvids have large brains compared to other birds. Densely packed with nerve cells, the large inner portion of the forebrain is the center for the storing and processing of information. An ample forebrain is important for learning and for spatial memory, two qualities that enable these birds to discriminate among similar objects and to live in very different environments.

Ravens are thought to store knowledge in the form of search images, evidenced by their habit of caching, or storing, food. Predators such as ravens form mental images of desired prey, as well as the locations of stashed treats, which assists them in detecting food. Other intelligent beings—most notably humans—are known to stockpile food as well. Climbers on high mountain peaks often bury foodstuffs in the snow for use on their downward descent. In order to re-find these caches, hikers use stakes and flags. Ever-resourceful ravens have been found excavating beneath these human-laid markers in order to score a meal. The questions here are: Did the birds learn the meaning of the stakes and flags? Or did they just accidentally happen upon one cache and then learn to associate food with the markers? Let's hope these wise guys don't figure out how to pilfer those six-packs of beer that we leave in cold running streams for enjoyment at the end of a long day out of doors.

A corvid of the forests of New Caledonia in the South Pacific, the New Caledonian Crow, is rather unusual in that it uses plant material—sticks, twigs, and even leaves—to probe under bark or crevices in order to obtain choice food items such as grubs and insects. Often the birds work over twigs to shape the ends into hooks, an effective tool for gleaning tasty treats from hard-to-reach locations. Under various conditions, a New Caledonian Crow in captivity was found to extend this tool-making capability to different materials. Provided with pieces of straight wire, the bird worked the wire until the ends were hooked and then used its new tool to extract food from a vertical pipe. Modifying previously unknown objects into functional tools certainly indicates a high level of intelligence.

In another example of this brain power, the New Caledonian Crow sometimes uses serrated leaves as tools for gathering food. Researchers studying these leafy tools discovered that the birds preferred to make notches on the left edges of the leaves, indicating use of the right eye and the right side of the bill. Right dominance or bias was previously thought to be a trait exclusive to human beings.

Cognition in animals is something that some scientists don't always recognize. Because the thought processes of birds cannot be directly observed, the only way to study them is through observation of their behavior. Actions are then interpreted by the observer(s). Thus hard-and-fast conclusions are difficult to reach. Whatever processes are involved here, it does seem likely that corvids would score high on their SATs.

Aerial Artists

If a raven cry just o'er head, some in the towne
have lost their maidenhead.

—TRADITIONAL BRITISH RHYME

WHETHER IT'S SPEED, ACROBATICS, or ballet, Common Ravens are masters of all genres. These aerodynamically streamlined creatures can shoot down valley and vale with great swiftness, then ascend ridges and mountains with effortless grace. With fluid yet powerful wing beats, they can regularly fly between thirty and forty miles per hour. They undoubtedly attain much greater speeds when engaging in their legendary downward dives. Their wing beats are so strong that an audible "swooshing" sound may be heard. Ravens are able to alternate flapping and gliding, and they may also soar to great heights. These large-bodied birds can remain stationary in the

sky even in the midst of a strong gale. Flapping, gliding, and soaring are punctuated with impressive acrobatic feats, giving the impression that these birds absolutely love to fly.

The same aerodynamic forces that apply to airplanes in flight also apply to flying birds—lift and drag. The outer section of each wing has strong, pliable feathers, called primaries, which function a bit like propellers when a bird takes to the air. The bird's tail aids in steering and helps with landing as well.

Combing the wind with fingered wings, ravens are powerful aerialists capable of flying for mile after mile. The pronounced fingers, or slottings, on their wings are gaps between the primary feathers and provide extra lift, essential for large birds. Coupled with their relatively long, narrow wings, it's easy to see why they are able to cover great distances, an essential skill for locating carcasses that are usually widely spaced.

Ravens differ from other members of the passerine family, which generally fly short distances to snag an insect, pick a fruit or seed, or work along the limbs and branches of trees in order to glean larvae. Demonstrating fierce speed and agility, the adaptable raven flies far and wide in its quest for food.

Common Ravens are generally year-round residents in most locations and do not migrate. However, certain environmental conditions may cause some individual ravens to wander seasonally, searching for food or water, and a single bird may fly more than 150 miles in a year's time. The home range of a raven's breeding territory is large, anywhere from 200 acres to nearly 10,000.

With the onset of the breeding season ravens become even more frolicsome, performing steep nosedives combined with a great deal of rolling and whirling about. They may also perform chases and aerial battles with other birds that are perceived as territorial intruders. Breeding pairs often soar, swoop, and tumble over and over together in midair, sometimes flying in tandem with their wing tips touching. The late Lawrence Kilham recalls in his title, *The American Crow and the Common Raven*, "I saw a pair of ravens flying wing tip to wing tip, lazily circling and drifting, rising and falling, with one sometimes swooping gently on the other."

Known for their stirring aerial displays, often performed in pairs or trios, ravens frolic and wheel through space. These consummate flyers perform lofty maneuvers sometimes in large groups, which are undoubtedly associated with mating rituals, pair bonding, establishing dominance, and, often, simply for play.

Especially thrilling to watch are the ravens' precipitous downward dives. With wings folded and closed, they plunge downward with amazing speed, and after plummeting hundreds of feet, suddenly pull up, rolling and tumbling in the process.   Some have nicknamed these birds "hell divers." Like overactive stunt pilots, they exhibit great maneuverability and can change directions very quickly. Ravens have been noted to fly briefly (a few seconds) in a completely inverted position—i.e., upside down.

The barrel roll is a maneuver in which the bird rotates on its longitudinal axis while maintaining its original direction in flight, an impressive feat indeed. Series of somersaults may also be performed, with the birds rolling their bodies in tight circles, their feet over their heads.

Ever playful, the rollicking Common Raven sometimes drops an item of food or a stick from a high cliff and then plunges downward to see if it can catch the object before it hits the ground. Flying is clearly a means of expression—in this case playfulness—but it is also a way of showing off to potential mates.

Since ravens are able to remain aloft without flapping their wings, they take advantage of rising currents of warm air, called thermals, to tower upward in the sky. Sometimes dozens of ravens will form "kettles," using thermals to gain altitude. The sight of a group of ravens soaring on updrafts is thought to look like water boiling in a kettle, hence the name. This is probably a means of attaining higher vantage points for searching for food.

Common Ravens molt completely once a year, shedding their old, worn feathers and growing new ones. In most birds, this process commences following the nesting season. However, in hefty-sized species such as ravens, the casting and renewal of primary feathers may begin earlier in the spring. Because ravens fly such long distances on an almost daily basis, as they explore for food, molting of the larger primary feathers proceeds rather slowly; this adaptation ensures that their flying ability is never totally impaired.

Ravenous Ravens

There were three ravens sat on a tree,
They were as black as they might be.
The one of them said to his make [mate],
Where shall we our breakfast take?

—FROM THE BALLAD
"THE THREE RAVENS," CIRCA 1611

A VENERABLE MAN FROM THE KOYUKON TRIBE of northern Alaska reportedly told the following to the author of *Make Prayers to the Raven*, Richard K. Nelson: "You know, raven don't hunt anything for himself. He gets his food the lazy way, just watches for whatever he can find already dead."

It's easy to see why this perception might exist. Ravens routinely scavenge from animal carcasses killed by other predators. But their feeding behavior is almost as diverse as their diet. These opportunistic birds make off with sled-dog food in northerly climes; steal bagels out of backpacks almost anywhere; raid unattended grocery sacks; snag insects, rodents, bird eggs and nestlings, fruits and grains; dine on dead meat; and grab garbage whenever it's available. To put it mildly, they are gustatorily versatile.

The heavy-duty, all-purpose bill of the raven enables it to pick fruits, rip flesh, carry off smashed bugs, spirit away eggs from other birds' nests, and probe into holes and crevices among bones or rocks. The upper bill is slightly hooked at the end, useful for ripping off pieces of flesh. In order to consume large eggs, ravens use their sharp, pointed lower mandibles (the lower half of a bird's bill, akin to the lower jaw in humans) to perforate the eggshell. Knocking off fragments around the punctured areas, they are eventually able to reach inside the egg to yank out the tasty innards. When food is scarce, these resourceful birds may eat the scat from wolves

Sample Raven Menu

Grasshoppers	Eggs	Cultivated grains
Beetles	Young desert tortoises	Acorns
Caterpillars		Berries
Army worms	Young and wounded birds	Garbage
Rodents	Afterbirth of lambs and calves	Insects and berries from scat
Lizards		
Frogs	Dead and decaying flesh	
Fish		

and bears, which usually contains nutrient-rich berries. They may also feed on cow dung.

The garbage dump is a raven's dream. Refuse heaps provide bits and pieces of all kinds of delectable food items. They probably also hold great appeal because of the birds' inherent curiosity. Resourceful ravens have learned that overflowing dumpsters or trash bins offer a choice selection of delicious treats. Whether it's French fries or the remains of a hamburger garnered from a fast-food dumpster located along a major interstate, or a piece of fruit from a Costco trash can, almost anything edible suits this versatile diner.

It's not just human trash bins that attract ravens. These streetwise scavengers also methodically fly along highways and byways, searching for road kills—animals, birds, and insects that have been

hit by moving automobiles. Interestingly, ravens have been seen taking in salts along icy roads in more northerly climes. The road salts are generally mixed with sand, and the gritty mixture may serve as a digestive aid. Roadways and other hard surfaces are also useful for cracking open certain comestible items. Nuts, clams, and crabs are most easily broken by dropping them on asphalt or rocks or off cliffs. The astute raven seems to be uncannily capable of judging the proper height for release in order to ensure just the proper amount of breakage for any given food item. For softer bits of food that require breaking up, ravens use their strong feet to secure the tidbit, then hammer away at it with their bills.

In addition to scavenging, ravens are also skilled predators, hunting for rodents in fields and stealing nestlings from other birds' nests. They often plunder entire broods of helpless ducklings. They've been known to seize doves and ducks in flight, and to snatch pigeons and flickers from their nests. Young desert tortoises make munchy meals and are particularly vulnerable in the Mojave Desert of southern California, where raven populations have increased significantly since the 1970s. Sadly, desert tortoises, the largest native land turtles in North America, are federally listed as a threatened species. Adults can reach one foot long and weigh up to nine pounds, but hatchling tortoises are tiny, a mere two inches in length. The shells of the baby tortoises are soft until about five or six years of age, making puncture wounds relatively easy. Coupled with their slow movements, the youngsters are extremely vulnerable to predation. And sharp-eyed ravens seem to have an uncanny ability to locate these tiny creatures.

To determine the impact of raven predation upon the tortoises, researchers have been conducting studies in the Mojave Desert using artificial baits—two-inch Styrofoam models, fabricated to look like baby tortoises. Baits were placed in locations that would be visible to birds flying overhead. After a period of time, the "Styro" babies were retrieved and checked for puncture marks. Out of 100 baits, researchers found twenty-nine punctures in the distinctive shape of the raven's bill. Interestingly, there were no signs of attacks by any other animals. Researchers found that areas around landfills posed the most risk for the young tortoises; in fact, there was nearly a 100 percent predation rate in those areas—undoubtedly due to the concentration of ravens in one of their favorite haunts.

In western Alaska, these black bandits have been seen pirating the eggs of Common Murres, seagoing birds that come to land only to nest. After alighting near an incubating murre, the cheeky raven, with its powerful beak, plucks the adult from its nest, grabs an egg, and then flies off to enjoy the feast. Ravens are also known to pick up and drop sticks, clods of dirt, and other objects upon nesting gulls in order to flush them from their egg clutches. One story describes a raven dropping a paper sack, crumpled up to make more of an impact, on a child who was holding a bag of French fries.

Relationships with Other Animals

Despite their large, stout bills, ravens are not able to open the corpses of big dead animals. As a result, they rely on other creatures to perform this function, often keeping company with grizzly and polar bears, wolves, coyotes, killer whales, mountain lions, and humans—creatures that guarantee a meal ticket. The birds may follow hunting carnivores until a kill is made, or follow potential prey and wait until one dies off. Historically, ravens followed the Vikings for the same reason they now trail wolves during caribou migrations—the urgency of locating food in order to ensure their own survival. With sharp eyes and wide-ranging habits, ravens are also good at leading coyotes or wolves to prey, ensuring that flesh will be torn apart and a feed will ensue. This symbiosis between animals benefits both bird and mammal. One partner provides the other with a service that increases the ability of both to secure food, and thus to survive. The late R. D. Lawrence, naturalist and wildlife author, memorably noted that, "Nothing is more haunting, spiritual, and primitive than the calls of ravens and wolves coming at the same time from the same location, a wild concert not infrequently heard during the breeding season of wolves and after a pack has made a kill."

Ravens often communicate vocally to others in their clan to reveal the location of food sources. They also perform soaring aerial displays as a way of moving their roosting mates closer to a dead animal. Upon approaching a carcass, the excited birds may engage in a dance, leaping and frisking about. This may be from nervousness, a cautionary behavior, or simply a way to celebrate the thrill of locating a meal. After tearing off chunks of meat from a carcass, birds fly off to eat or take food to share with nestlings or a mate, or they may find a secret hiding place to store the meat for later consumption.

Relationships with Humans

Ravens and crows have always had a strong connection with human cultures, with food at the heart of it all. During the Pleistocene era, the scavenging birds were able to feed on dead animals and the decaying flesh of large animals, hunted and killed by human beings. They also learned how to steal fish caught by early fisherman, since the fish were often left out in plain sight to dry. Obviously their thievery could not be overlooked, and the necessity for driving them off from sources of food may have encouraged people to work more cooperatively and to live in groups—so theorize John M. Marzluff and Tony Angell in their 2005 book titled *In the Company of Crows and Ravens.* The birds, sensing human resistance to their presence, began to develop a certain wariness of man. Although corvids were a threat to their food supplies, humans also noted the birds' rather mysterious natures and were impressed by their tenacity and innovativeness in terms of stealing food. This made ravens and crows ideal cultural icons, and they became the subject of much folklore and legend.

In part because of their close association with death, ravens also became objects of worship. From the Middle Ages until the late nineteenth century, many battles and wars ensued, which created an abundance of corpses—providing a plethora of food for corvids. The presence of the birds in and around battlegrounds made for increased proximity to man and, understandably, led to some rather negative attitudes about these all-black "death" birds.

This gloomy negativity was further reinforced when it became apparent that ravens and crows enjoyed dining on agricultural crops meant to feed human beings. And so persecution of these birds began, and ravens and crows were hunted down. The use of scarecrows became commonplace in both field and garden in an attempt to fend off the marauding birds. As the birds were increasingly harassed, they became more shy and wary, passed along these traits to their offspring, and developed cooperation among their own kind.

As noted above, for centuries ravens have been persecuted by farmers and gardeners because of their affinity for eating cultivated grains. Along with their crow cousins, ravens have been blamed for the failure of numerous crops. Creative farmers have used a variety of materials to create devices for discouraging hungry birds. Most notable is the scarecrow. Also called jack-of-straw, scarebird, tattie-bogle, shoy-hoy, tattie-doolie, and Jack O'Kent, these crude effigies have been used for more than 3,000 years in an attempt to dissuade birds from eating the crops of hardworking farmers. However, while ravens may eat some items growing in the local cornfield or vegetable patch, they also feast on grubs, caterpillars, army worms, and other agricultural pests. Researchers who have examined the innards of these birds have discovered that they contained bounteous amounts of grasshoppers—a good thing for farmers.

Despite all this persecution and negativity, humans have always recognized the raven as a kindred spirit, possessing many qualities similar to their own. And ravens have become part of many cultures through art and literature, as well as music and film. Today in our increasingly urban society, we inadvertently encourage town life for ravens by amassing food scraps in landfills and trash receptacles. Corvid numbers in many cities are on the increase as a result.

Food Storage

As with other members of the corvid family, ravens cache, or stockpile, food to be eaten at a later time—an efficient means of making use of food sources that are available only temporarily. This behavior is probably related to a perception that food supplies are limited in nature, and that there are many other creatures vying for the same resources. The instinctive urge to stockpile extends to curious young ravens who, only a few days out of the nest, begin stashing away edible items—as well as inedible objects. (Even adult ravens have been known to squirrel away an inanimate golf ball or two.)

Ravens hoard a variety of food items throughout the year, hiding them in the ground, under or between rocks, beneath leaves, or under mounds of snow. Chunks of food are held in the raven's bill or throat, often having first been brought up from deep within the gullet. The bird pokes its bill into a chosen repository and, with the aid of its tongue, expels the food. After withdrawing the bill, it rakes soil and/or plant material over the spot, using a sideways motion of the beak. Stones or leaves are sometimes placed atop the stash site. Ravens are occasionally choosey about how they overlay their cache sites, moving about to find the ideal covering for their treasures. These masters of deception sometimes try to fool other creatures that might attempt to plunder their food stockpiles. After going through the motions of placing a bit of food in one area, they may then decide to pick it up with their bills and speedily fly away to hide the delicacy elsewhere.

How long these birds remember the location of their layaways is up for speculation. Some studies indicate that there is a decline in memory after a few weeks. But the ability to memorize the whereabouts of food repositories may not be that critical. Food items sometimes rot or are pilfered by other animals. The generalist raven seemingly has all-inclusive tastes. Couple that with their wandering ways and apparent ability to problem-solve, and we can probably safely speculate that they can afford to forget the locations of their stashes, because there is almost always something else around to eat.

All members of the corvid family are thought to partake of water on a regular basis. The wide-ranging raven seems to be able to readily locate water sources, drinking from puddles, lakes, streams, and cattle and irrigation troughs, as well as from farm sprinklers. The late Lawrence Kilham, a fellow of the American Ornithologists' Union and professor of microbiology, hand-raised a young raven that had fallen from a nest. He observed "Raveny" collecting in its mouth a small amount of water from a puddle and then flying a short distance to dump it on the roof of his house. On another occasion the frolicsome bird carried water from a pond and tossed it against the windshield of a car. Other observers report adult birds collecting and carrying water to quench the thirst of their young nestlings, particularly in dry climates. Moisture is also obtained from the juicy insects and fruits that ravens consume.

The omnivorous, opportunistic raven is a generalist when it comes to food, able to recognize and exploit many different resources. Because of its wide-ranging tastes, the raven must continually discriminate between quite an array of comestible items—in effect, keeping a running inventory of many different foods. This requires special traits such as inquisitiveness, curiosity, perception, ingenuity, and recollection, characteristics that other critters don't necessarily have. Birds and animals with more specialized eating requirements are able to survive with a lot less mental faculty because they need to identify only a few preferred food items.

Famous Ravens

And the Raven, never flitting, still is sitting, still is sitting
On the pallid bust of Pallas just above my chamber door;
And his eyes have all the seeming of a demon's that is dreaming,
And the lamplight o'er him streaming throws his shadow on the floor;
And my soul from out that shadow that lies floating on the floor
Shall be lifted—nevermore!

—from "The Raven,"
Edgar Allan Poe,
published January 1845

FEW BIRDS ARE AS ACCLAIMED AS THE RAVEN in Edgar Allan Poe's masterpiece poem. One of the most popular lyrical poems in the world, "The Raven" was written in 1844. Poe was a brooding, intense individual who was fascinated by the mystery and terror of death.

Nouns and adjectives used by Poe in "The Raven" evoke striking images of these mysterious birds: "ebony bird," "ancient," "ominous," "bird of yore," "prophet," "thing of evil." Despite the title of the poem, it is not about ravens, but rather about the great sadness associated with losing a loved one. The omniscient bird appears as a messenger to a man who has lost his lady love to the arms of death. The message from the all-knowing raven: The only way the man could be reunited with his lovely Lenore was through death.

Raven at the Tower of London.

Gregarious Guardians

Nearly as renowned as the bird in Poe's elegy are the Tower of London ravens. Their story dates to the seventeenth century. At that time, ravens were relatively common in the vicinity. According to the legend, flocks of these loquacious birds alerted royal guards to an attempted raid on the tower by Oliver Cromwell, when the birds carried on in such a disturbed manner that the Tower guards were alerted in time to save the day.

Although regarded as heroes on that particular day, ravens were generally unpopular with Londoners because of their propensity for dining on the bodies of human beings. The ravens were performing much-needed janitorial services by feasting on city garbage, but Londoners ignored that virtue and once petitioned King Charles II that the macabre creatures be eradicated. Charles, however, was forewarned that if he eliminated all of the ravens a disaster of massive proportions would befall England, including the destruction of his royal palace. Not wishing to tempt fate, nor wishing to lose his own home, Charles decreed that at least half a dozen ravens should be kept as guardians of the Tower of London.

Some people deride this story as complete myth, charging that there is scant evidence that ravens were actually kept in the Tower before the 1800s. However, many continue to believe in the legend. While wild ravens no longer live in or around London, six to eight birds, entrusted to a yeoman ravenmaster, are still kept at the Tower of London. The birds live comfortably and continue to be regarded with great respect. Yeoman Derrick Coyle from the Tower noted during an interview with the BBC that he "wouldn't have it any other way. The ravens are a part of the family. They all have their own characters—they're very intelligent and mischievous."

Over the years, thousands of people have enjoyed visiting and watching the Tower birds. Russian President Vladimir Putin was charmed during his visit to the Tower of London by receiving a verbal greeting, uttered from shiny, black beaks. Unfortunately, in recent years, the birds have been taken off display and sequestered in the inner sanctum because of concerns about avian flu.

Tower of London

The Tower of London was founded in 1066 by William the Conqueror. This magnificent structure has served as an arsenal, fortress, jewel house, prison and place of execution, menagerie, mint, and royal palace. The smallest population of ravens resided here during World War II, when only one bird lived in the Tower. Since that time, there have been at least six ravens in residence. The inquisitive birds occasionally escape from the Tower, despite wing clippings, and sometimes they are excused for bad behavior. Jim Crow was the oldest raven to live in the Tower of London; he lived to be forty-four years of age.

WHAT THE TOWER RAVENS ARE FED:

blood-soaked biscuits

boiled eggs (including shell)

raw meat (beef, pork, liver, lambs' heart, rabbit)

Natural Navigators

An aptitude for locating terra firma has been attributed to ravens since time immemorial. The raven was reportedly the first creature to be sent from Noah's ark to look for land. According to Genesis 8: 6–7:

> And it came to pass at the end of forty days, that
> Noah opened the window of the ark which he
> had made:
> And he sent forth a raven, which went forth to
> and from until the waters were dried up from off
> the earth.

Unfortunately, Noah's raven did not return to the ark, and it was assumed that the bird had discovered land with plenty of dining opportunities. (As an aside, in Jewish legend, ravens were looked down upon because they continually defied a decree against lovemaking on the ark.)

In 1750 B.C., ancient Babylonian sailors reportedly followed these birds, confident that they would lead them to land. The Roman scholar and naturalist Pliny the Elder reported that Ceylonese mariners kept ravens on their ships and set their course by following the paths of these excellent navigators.

The Vikings capitalized on the navigational skills of the raven as well. In A.D. 874, a Norwegian explorer by the name of Floki set out to find a large island to the west of Norway. The possibility that there was an actual land mass to the west had been reported some ten years earlier by a Swedish explorer named Gardar. According to the *Saga of Floki*, three ravens were brought along on the quest. Floki released the first raven. It did not return, and he assumed that it had flown back to Norway. The second bird was released and later returned to the ship, apparently not finding land. The third raven flew in a westward direction and never returned; it had apparently discovered land with many food sources. Floki (later nicknamed Raven-Floki) elected to follow the route of raven number three. And, according to the saga, this is how the Vikings discovered the southeast coast of Iceland. To this day, ravens are respected and revered in Iceland—at least for the most part. In places in Iceland where the feathery down from eider ducks is gathered for commercial purposes, ravens are considered dastardly pests because they eat the ducks' eggs and young nestlings.

Astute Advisors

The Norse deity Odin, an impressive being indeed, was the god of wisdom, art, culture, war, and the deceased, not to mention being the supreme deity and creator of human beings and the cosmos— interestingly, some of the very same characteristics attributed to ravens in some cultures. Extraordinary as he sounds, Odin apparently owed some of his success to a pair of keen-eyed, all-seeing ravens. One was named Hugin, and it embodied thought; the other was

ODIN'S RAVENS

Hugin and Munin
fly every day
over the great earth;
I fear for Hugin,
that he may not return,
yet more am I anxious
for Munin.

—FROM GRIMNISMÁL, AN ICELANDIC EPIC POEM IN THE
THIRTEENTH-CENTURY MEDIEVAL MANUSCRIPT CODEX REGIUS,
TRANSLATED FROM OLD NORSE BY RASMUS B. ANDERSON, 1876

called Munin, and it represented memory. At dawn each day, Odin would send his two ravens out to see what was happening in the world. After flying far and wide, Hugin and Munin would return in the evening, perch on Odin's shoulders and share with him the secrets they had learned. The ravens were considered ideal messengers because of their discerning eyes, razor-sharp intelligence, and astute memory, as well as their ability to fly great distances. Odin was confident that nothing would be overlooked by Hugin and Munin. Supplied with information from his avian counselors, Odin then passed along words of wisdom and advice to the other Norse gods.

In tribute to this legend, the Oslo, Norway, city hall is adorned with wooden reliefs showing the great Odin with his two ravens.

Predictors of Weather

In addition to possessing the ability to locate dry land, ravens in some cultures were believed to dictate the weather; people also believed that rain fell only after one of the birds was killed. The Greek philosopher Theophrastus, who lived from 371 to 286 B.C., wrote:

> It is a sign of rain if the raven, who is accustomed to make many different sounds, repeats one of these twice quickly and makes a whirring sound and shakes his wings. So too if, during a rainy season, he utters many different sounds, or if he searches for lice perched on an olive tree. And if, whether in fair or wet weather, he imitates, as it were, with his voice, falling drops, it is a sign of rain.

Birds of Darkness

To see one raven is lucky, 'tis true,
But it's certain misfortune to light upon two
And meeting with three is the devil!

—FROM THE BALLAD
"BILL JONES," M. G. LEWIS, 1808

FROM THE TIP OF ITS BILL TO THE END OF ITS TAIL, the Common Raven is as black as night, and the bird has a somewhat sinister reputation accordingly. Sometimes when the light shines just right, the feathers show a burnish of iridescent greens, blues, purples, and silver. It turns out that there are certain practical advantages to being the color of the night.

Advantages to the Color Black

For birds there are physiological and social benefits to the color black. Dark skin and feathers are effective for absorbing solar heat, enabling ravens to live and thrive in extremely cold climates. In Arctic climates where nighttime temperatures sometimes reach minus-58 degrees Fahrenheit, sunny days make all the difference. A bird positions itself toward the sun and erects the feathers on its head, belly, flanks, and rump. By so doing, it exposes its feathers as well as its dark skin to the sun, maximizing heat absorption. Heat from solar radiation helps to reduce energy requirements.

Although their black tincture might be considered a disadvantage in extremely hot climates, the adaptable ravens cope in other ways: they forage for food in open, sun-drenched country either very early or late in the day, when temperatures are more bearable. Black feathers also tend to be stronger and less susceptible to wear and tear than less pigmented feathers. Black coloration makes ravens more conspicuous during the daytime; if individuals are easily seen and recognized by fellow ravens, social interactions are more likely to be successful.

During the nighttime hours, their jet-black tones enable ravens to blend into the darkness, protecting them from predators such as owls. Cryptic coloration also makes it easier for these shadowy birds to sneak up on prey.

Symbols of Death and Destruction

Throughout history, crows and ravens have been associated with destruction, death, and the afterlife—in part because of their color, but also because of their ghoulish feeding habits. In general,

corvids were regarded as vermin in Europe from the 1700s to early 1900s; bounties were placed on their heads, and many nests were destroyed.

In contrast to the beliefs in Europe, in Tibet ravens and crows were regarded as messengers for the Supreme Being, and as such, thought to be particularly important at funeral sacraments. During these traditional ceremonies, a deceased individual was dissected into bite-sized portions and placed on an altar. Crows and ravens, as well as other scavengers, would then seize and spirit away the fragments to the afterlife. According to some shamans elsewhere in Asia, the croaking of a raven is not just a sign of the news of someone's death but actually represents the speech of the deceased—the soul of the dead speaking from the afterworld.

In various Pacific Northwest cultures—including the Tlingit and Haida—headgear included the feathers of ravens and crows. Wearing headwear with corvid feathers was believed to enable the feather-bedecked individuals to journey into the land of the dead and return with a person's soul; this was a way of bringing back a loved one.

There are many references to ravens at battlegrounds, sites of bravery and death. Viking warriors carried sacred ravens into battle, so the victims of the formidable Vikings dreaded the sight of the large black birds because of their association with invasion and murder. Celtic battle helmets from Romania were reportedly topped with iron ravens whose wings flapped as the warriors entered battle. Throughout the ninth, tenth, and eleventh centuries, rulers of Scandinavian countries possessed war banners shaped like ravens. It was believed that when the banners appeared to be flying, victory awaited, but when the flags were lifeless, defeat was sure to follow. William the Conqueror also carried "villainous" ravens on his campaigns, and the birds make a grisly appearance in the old English poem called "The Battle of Brunanburh":

> They left behind them, to enjoy feasting on the corpses,
> the dark-coated one, the swart raven, with the horny beak.

The horny beak refers to the Roman nose, or high bridge, on the bill of the raven.

The association between ravens and fatalities, either from war, illness, or execution, led to the theory that the birds were able to foretell death. The birds' verbal declarations, hoarse and croaking, were thought to portend impending calamity in many parts of Africa, Asia, and Europe. In many areas of the ancient world, the sight of a raven flying to the right was considered a good omen; if a bird was seen flying to the left it foreboded evil. The Scottish goddess of winter, Cailleach, sometimes appeared as a raven, and her touch brought death. Morrigan, the Celtic goddess of war, death, prophecy, and passionate love, sometimes appeared as a black raven who fed on deceased warriors following battle.

The old English term "ravenstone" indicates a place of execution, and tombstones are sometimes called ravenstones. In German, an evil person who deserves to hang is still called a *Rabenaas,* meaning "raven carrion." During the fourteenth-century outbreaks of the Black Death, a form of bubonic plague pandemic throughout Europe and much of Asia, medical doctors went from house to house wearing helmets that resembled crow or raven heads. Aromatic colognes were placed in the large "beaks" of the helmets in order to offset the redolence of moldering flesh. And, of course, there is the Poe poem that speaks to the death of Lenore.

On a more positive note, these dark birds have also been regarded as symbols of good luck and fortune, and associated with healing as well. Deer-hunting Scottish highlanders considered a calling raven a sign of good luck. The Irish expected good luck if they heard a raven croaking and if it flew to the viewer's right side. The Koyukon and other Arctic peoples believed that if they prayed properly to ravens, successful hunting would ensue. Many hunters offered these prayers because they felt that the birds would reveal the whereabouts of elk, deer, and caribou. Divine ravens were thought to place spells on certain prey, holding them down long enough for humans to make the kill. In return for their services, of course, these resourceful birds always expected to share in the meal.

Shamans from the Koyukon tribe of northern Alaska attempted to call forth the power of the raven in hopes of curing disease. By imitating the bird's calls and spreading their arms to look like wings, these powerful medicine men believed they could heal the sick.

Black or White?

Legend has it that crows and ravens were once white. According to one Greek myth, Apollo—the god of prophecy, medicine, music, and poetry—turned the crow into its present ink-black color after the bird told him that his mistress had wed another.

A Vietnamese fable tells of two bird companions, a white raven and a white peacock, who one day decided to entertain themselves by painting each other's feathers. The creative raven set to work and masterfully painted the peacock in the dazzling hues of the rainbow so that it was, and remains, one of the most stunning birds on earth. The peacock, however, did not feel particularly generous. Unwilling to share its newfound glory, the peacock painted the raven an uninspiring black.

The color change in an Inuit (Eskimo) tale goes something like this: The owl and the raven were good pals, and to show this, the raven made a new dress for the owl; the dress was black and white. The owl wanted to give its friend something in return, so first it crafted a pair of boots, made of whalebone. Then the owl began to make the raven a white dress. Since the owl wanted the dress to fit perfectly, it asked the raven to remain motionless for a fitting. But the raven began hopping about and would not sit still. The owl got angry and said, "If I fly over you with a blubber lamp, don't jump." The raven continued to be agitated and to hop about. This was the last straw for the owl, so it emptied a blubber lamp filled with its blackish substance over the new white dress. The raven, of course, cried out because the dress was ruined. But ever since that day, the raven has been black all over.

North American Pueblo tribes have their own stories about the changeover from white to black. At Zuni Pueblo, crows reportedly had white shoulder bands until two Zuni warriors offered to share a smoke with a certain crow. The hoggish bird inhaled such a deep, strong puff that the smoke stained all of its feathers black.

At Hopi, there is a different tale: A young Kachina boy soaked sunflower seeds in water, turning the liquid black. He then poured the sooty water on the white crow and made it the color of obsidian.

At Acoma Pueblo the legend is connected to the volcano demon: "Crow was snow-white. He tried to beat out the fire with his wings and he was changed by the heat till he became black."

The Haida name for raven was Yaahl, and the original Yaahl was white. In Aboriginal mythology, a white raven reportedly tried to steal fire from the Seven Sisters (the star cluster known as the Pleiades) and was singed soot-black in its unsuccessful attempt.

Some of these legends may have originated from sightings of albinistic birds, those with white feathers instead of the usual black. White feathers may cover an entire bird, although this is rare. True albinos lack any pigmentation whatsoever and have pink or red eyes and pale or white feet, legs, and bills. They tend to have weak eyesight and brittle feathers on both the wings and tail. Total albinism is caused by a genetic change that inhibits the formation of the enzyme responsible for pigment synthesis. Partial albinism, in which only certain feathers lack pigmentation, is much more common. Corvids are born featherless, and dietary or circulatory deficiencies occurring at the time of feather development may cause white coloration. Patches of abnormally white feathers on an otherwise normally colored bird may be the result of injury. It is also possible that aberrant feathers may crop up each year as new feathers grow in as part of the molting process.

Beyond "Nevermore"

Then, upon the velvet sinking, I betook myself to linking
Fancy unto fancy, thinking what this ominous bird of yore—
What this grim, ungainly, ghastly, gaunt and ominous bird of yore
Meant in croaking "Nevermore."

—FROM "THE RAVEN," EDGAR ALLAN POE,
PUBLISHED JANUARY 1845

"Nevermore" barely touches upon the vocal repertoire of the Common Raven. These loquacious birds have some of the most complex vocabularies in the avian world. Although classified as songbirds, ravens are hardly melodious, but they do have many different calls. They croak, scream, knock, yell, caw, and trill, just to describe a few.

Part of every Common Raven's repertoire is the characteristic croaking *quork*, and a metallic *tok*, usually given when other birds

The raven appears in Haida culture, represented here on a totem pole.

are flying over. They also mimic the sounds of other animals and people, as well as inanimate objects. Some of their vocalizations can be likened to the chiming of wood blowing in a strong wind, the pealing of church bells, or the sound of water dripping into a metal pan. In Europe, the "knocking" sound of ravens is similar to the mating calls of another large bird, the white stork. Birds reared in isolation have been taught to mimic a variety of sounds, including "nevermore."

Nobel prize–winning behavioral scientist Konrad Lorenz had a pet raven that learned to mimic its own name, Roah. Whenever the raven perceived that its master was in some sort of danger, it would fly away from the peril and call *roah, roah, roah* repeatedly as a way of luring its master to safety.

In general, the vocalizations of Common Ravens are hoarse, resounding, and penetrating, and they always seem to demand our attention. The Bella Bella tribe of British Columbia paid tribute to the raven as the "one whose voice is to be obeyed," obviously a reference to its strong, resonant cry. In ancient Ireland, future events (good fortune, impending disaster) were divined from the calls of the raven.

These multivoiced birds have an incredible repertoire of calls, varying in intensity, duration, pitch, and rate. Various studies have recorded anywhere from twelve to more than thirty different calls in individual birds, some with multiple syllables and regional dialects. Of course bird calls are always subject to human interpretation, and anecdotal descriptions vary considerably from one person or culture to the next. Different calls carry different messages.

For example, a short, high-pitched alarm-call *keck-keck-keck* may be delivered when a raptor flies overhead. When a bird is being chased, the calls are very choppy and high-pitched. According to zoologist Bernrd Heinrich, the birds are particularly rackety at food baits, yelling and carrying on, probably alerting other ravens to the availability of a meal. The yell call probably evolved from the begging calls of fledgling birds upon spotting an adult carrying food.

Vocalizations are particularly important for birds, such as ravens, that are uniformly one color, for it is probably difficult to recognize close kin from far away. Calls are a way of disclosing individual, group, or even family identity. Paired birds often coordinate their calling bouts in order to emphasize their territory and to keep track of one another, sometimes copying a few of each other's calls to ensure that they will recognize their partners. Raven nestlings utter high-pitched begging calls that become deeper and more raspy sounding by the time they leave the nest. Young birds often engage in babbling, gurgling monologues that may go on for an hour or more.

Ravens are clever vocalists, no doubt using verbalizations to indicate the presence of other birds in an area, who's courting whom, and the proximity of predators, danger, and food. But sometimes when flying far and wide, it is almost as if they are calling out with a resonant *quork* simply for the pure joy of it.

Rapturous Ravens

In the old age black was not counted fair,
Or if it were it bore not beauty's name;
But now is black beauty's successive heir...
Therefore my mistress' eyes are raven black.

—FROM "SONNET 127," WILLIAM SHAKESPEARE

IN THE AVIAN WORLD, males tend to be the more attractive and colorful of the two sexes. This makes sense from an evolutionary point of view because the duller the female, the less likely she is to be spotted as she sits on her nest or tends her young, thereby ensuring more reproductive success. Males of most species use their good looks to attract members of the opposite sex by displaying fancy markings or flashing colorful feathers. Where does this leave the Common Raven, a monochromatic bird the color of tar?

Courtship

As it turns out, males are perceived as anything but dull in the eyes of female ravens, because they have ways of turning on the charm despite having no colorful or smartly patterned markings. Sexual magnetism is achieved by raising certain feathers, moving wings and tails in suggestive fashion, and, believe it or not, by eye-flashing.

Many birds have thin transparent membranes that lie under the eyelids. When not in use, these so-called "second eyelids," or nictitating membranes, are tucked up in the corners of the eyes. The primary purpose of the nictitating membranes is to protect and moisturize the birds' eyeballs without completely shutting out

Common Raven with nictitating membrane visible on the eye.

light. This is particularly important for birds in flight because rushing, oncoming air quickly dries out the corneas. Male ravens are known to flash these pale membranes to indicate aggression as well as excitement. Imagine for just a moment the impact of flashing white eyes set against the pitch-black darkness of the rest of the bird—ravishing.

In order to look alluring, the male raven may raise the feathers above his eyes so that it looks as if he has two splendiferous ears. Then, by altering the position of the flank feathers, he suddenly looks to be wearing a pair of trousers. And, as if dandy trousers weren't enough, the male may then erect the feathers on his throat, neck, and breast to exaggerate his shaggy hackles. The sexy look is complete after he opens his wings slightly at the shoulders and puffs himself up with pride. Once the posture is achieved, he struts about in what he hopes is an impassioned manner, calling soothingly and bowing before the female. The eye flashing is icing on the cake. Hey, that tousled, dreamy-eyed look works for a lot of females, particularly when coupled with courtly bowing.

Males also perform aerial acrobatics to impress females, carrying on and showing off by swooping and tumbling in midair. Courting raven pairs often fly together, soaring high in the sky.

The jury is still out as to whether ravens mate for life, although many consider this a hallmark trait of the corvid family. But it is clear that established pairs often stay together, flying and hunting as a team. When perched they may touch bills and tenderly groom one another by probing and combing their feathers to remove irritants such as mites or flies, a practice known as allopreening.

Nest Sites

As with other aspects of their behavior, ravens are flexible in their choice of nesting locations. They often use trees, cliffs, or rocky headlands. For added protection, they may look for rock ledges with overhangs. However, they also select sites that are completely exposed to the elements. Man-made structures such as oil derricks, windmills, bridges, telephone poles, power-line towers, and even billboards are popular. Crossbars on these structures help to hold nests in place. Raven nests have been documented in deserted automobiles and other vehicles. There is even a report of a nest in a rusted-out barbecue occupying an old railroad car. Ravens sometimes use highway overpasses, and in large cities they may nest on high-rise buildings. The most important consideration for nest location is the availability of adequate food sources for feeding the young.

Nest Building

The female raven is the chief architect for nest construction, creating a bulky basket of large sticks and twigs with a deep depression in the center. Sticks are placed loosely on a platform, ledge, or crossbar, or may be wedged into the crotch of a good-sized tree. Nests are lined with numerous cushy materials that provide softness and warmth: leaves, feathers, moss, strips of bark, grass, animal hair, and sometimes mud, sheep's wool, paper, or old rags.

Males assist in the construction process by rounding up sticks and other materials and presenting them to the female. The type of plant material doesn't seem to be of concern; these flexible birds select twigs and branches from many different kinds of trees and shrubs. Some mated pairs will use the same nest site year after year, placing new branches and twigs on top of the old.

Once courtship, mating, and nest construction have been completed, the female lays anywhere from three to seven oval-shaped eggs, mottled with brown and olive green. She is the primary incubator, sitting on the eggs and applying her precious body heat for about twenty days until the chicks emerge. Birds living in warm desert climes may begin nesting in late winter, while in colder areas the breeding season may be delayed until early spring.

During the incubation period, the primary role of the male is to safeguard the female and the eggs. As sentinel, he guards against intruding predators such as unrelated ravens, eagles, or large owls, or other threats. He also hunts and brings back food to the incubating female. Common Ravens generally produce only one brood per year. However, if a clutch is lost early in the season from predation or exposure to a storm, a second breeding attempt may be made.

Gangly Gargoyles

Newly hatched raven chicks are born blind and without feathers, and they are not particularly attractive. They are thought by some to resemble freakish-looking gargoyles. Any unhatched eggs are eaten by the ever-opportunistic adults. Both parents hunt and supply food to satiate the appetites of the growing young, and the raucous begging may be heard for miles around.

The "gargoyles" develop quickly. At about three weeks, downy feathers—small, soft, and fluffy—have grown in, helping to insulate their bodies. Tail and wing feathers continue to grow. By about five weeks, the young are fully feathered and begin fitfully exercising their wings. They leave the nest, or fledge, somewhere between five and seven weeks of age. Juvenile ravens generally stay close to the nest for some time, and parents continue caring for them for several more months. Some young ravens leave to wander about and join up with other juveniles for feeding and roosting.

Ravens tend to live in small family and clan territorial groups, often spending years together. Juveniles and adolescents sometimes stay with their parents for two or three years, learning important skills for socialization and survival. Ravens also flock together for more efficient hunting, and there is safety in numbers. If danger is detected, birds can warn others in their groups with vocalizations.

Feeling Their Oats

The way a crow
Shook down on me
The dust of snow
From a hemlock tree

Has given my heart
A change of mood
And saved some part
Of a day I had rued

—"Dust of Snow," Robert Frost, 1923

Corvids are uncommonly playful birds. In the great white North, ravens and wolves play a type of tag game. The birds wait for the wolves to fall asleep and then pounce on them, pulling tails or ears, at which point a chase ensues as the irritated wolves try to catch the jeering ravens. This game doesn't seem to have any clear benefits for acquiring food or for ensuring survival, but it does appear to be entertaining for both animals. Ravens also sometimes chase wolves, flying here and there about their heads, just out of reach of their snapping jaws.

Other crow and raven games include dropping objects from the air and then swooping down to catch them, engaging in bouts of tug-of-war, and performing balancing acts on extremely flimsy branches. Some describe birds joyfully hanging upside down from limbs or branches. Young ravens are said to be the most playful of all. In her book *Bird Brains*, Candace Savage describes ravens amusing themselves by playing "king of the hill." One raven seeks out an elevated location and taunts its playmates by brandishing about a small object such as a stick. Other ravens then attempt to seize the object from the "king," thereby displacing him. In another instance, one individual raven decided, apparently on a whim, to slide down a bank of snow. Youngsters in the same social

group followed suit. Savage also describes a frolicking diversion created by a young raven and a domestic dog in which the two animals took turns chasing each other around the trunk of a tree.

Play is a way for young ravens to learn about their relationship to the environment, which in turn contributes to their adaptability and versatility. Both young and adult ravens, when feeling particularly sprightly, will fly high in the sky, performing double loops and barrel rolls, circling, wheeling, and tumbling through the air.

My favorite story comes from a rancher in Sonora, Mexico, who told me of a burn site that attracts these inquisitive birds. Apparently marijuana that is confiscated by the Federales (Mexican federal police) at the United States–Mexico border is routinely taken to an area of open country near my friend's ranch, where the contraband is burned. Ravens are attracted to the fire primarily because of the possibility of locating edible creatures that may be rousted by the flames. However, the birds have discovered that there is a little something more to this experience.

By using rising currents of warm air, ravens are able to effortlessly climb upward above the marijuana-rich haze. After soaring above the vapors for some time, the birds become even more frolicsome and frisky than usual, diving and twisting, and performing astonishing aerobatic feats. Evidently the ravens have learned that the fumes provide a pleasant feeling of euphoria, a "natural" high, as well as the opportunity for dining on creatures fleeing the flames. They have stored the location of this site in their memory banks and continue to scan the skies for the first signs of these regular bonfires—a rave up to be sure.

Ravens in Literature

How sweetly did they float upon the wings
Of silence, through the empty-vaulted night,
At every fall smoothing the raven-down
Of darkness till it smiled!

—FROM *COMUS*, JOHN MILTON, 1634

RAVENS HAVE BEEN AN INTEGRAL PART OF LITERATURE for more than a millennium. From the Holy Bible to *Beowulf*, William Shakespeare, Edgar Allan Poe, and Charles Dickens, to fairy tales and Native American fables, the presence of these delightful birds in literary works is impressive indeed. While in many instances ravens symbolize evil, death, and doom in written works, there have also been allusions to their mischievous nature, their playfulness and sense of curiosity, their helpfulness, and their skills as shape-changers.

Early references to ravens occur in the Bible in numerous places, including Job 38:41: "Who provideth for raven his food? When his young ones cry unto God, they wander for lack of meat." In 1 Kings 17:2-6, the prophet Elijah is directed by the Lord to hide himself in a wilderness region near a brook by the name of Cherith. The Lord told Elijah that he would find safety and nourishment there:

> And it shall be, that thou shalt drink of the brook; and I
> have commanded the ravens to feed thee there.
> So he went and did according unto the word of the
> Lord: for he went and dwelt by the brook Cherith, that is
> before Jordan.
> And the ravens brought him bread and flesh in the
> morning, and bread and flesh in the evening; and he
> drank of the brook.

In this case, the raven is portrayed as a helpful, nurturing creature. Centuries later, the raven appears in the eighth-century Old English epic *Beowulf*:

> Therefore many a spear, cold in the morning, shall be
> grasped with fingers, raised by hands; no sound of harp
> shall waken the warriors, but the dark raven, low over the
> doomed, shall tell many tales, say to the eagle how he fared
> at the feast when with the wolf he spoiled the slain bodies.
>   —FROM *BEOWULF*, TRANSLATION BY M. H. ABRAMS, 1974

In this instance, the raven's role is very different from that with Elijah. Commonly described as the "beasts of battle," the raven, the wolf, and the eagle often appear in combat scenes in early literature. Recognized as scavengers, these three animals were thought to foreshadow future events, or to evoke emotion from the reader.

The presence of ravens at a battle scene appears again in a tenth- or eleventh-century Anglo-Saxon poem that retells a story from the Old Testament book of Judith:

> Linden shields clashed, resounded loud. The lean flanked
> wolves drooled in the woods and the dark raven, slaughter-
> greedy bird: they both perceived that the folk warriors
> went to provide for them their fill of doomed men.

—FROM "JUDITH," TRANSLATION
BY RICHARD M. TRASK, 1997

Because ravens were so frequently found near deceased humans, they were thought to be capable of foretelling death. In Shakespeare's *Macbeth,* Lady Macbeth hints at this in her speech when she finds out the king is coming for a visit: "The raven himself is hoarse/That croaks the fatal entrance of Duncan/Under my battlements." With the arrival of King Duncan into the home of Macbeth and Lady Macbeth, the husband and wife duo carry out their scheme for King Duncan's murder. In *Othello,* unwelcome news is compared to a raven flying "o'er the infected house." In *As You Like It,* Shakespeare wrote: "He that doth the ravens feed,/Yea, providently caters for the sparrow,/Be comfort to my age!" If the troublesome raven continues to thrive under God's watch, the character Adam trusts that even he will be cared for by God in his old age. In Sonnet 127, Shakespeare refers to a mistress's brow being "raven black," and in the play *Cymbeline,* the character Iachimo wishes for a dark morning: "Swift, swift, you dragons of the night, that dawning may bear the raven's eye."

Shakespeare's contemporaries also included the foreboding raven in their writings. In *The Jew of Malta* by English playwright Christopher Marlowe (1564–1593), the raven is considered an omen, a sign of bad things to come:

> Thus, like the sad-presaging raven that tolls
> The sick man's passport in her hollow beak,
> And in the shadow of the silent night
> Doth shake contagion from her sable wings,
> Vex'd and tormented runs poor Barabas
> With fatal curses towards these Christians.

The most famous work of English poet Edmund Spenser, another of Shakespeare's contemporaries (1552–1599), is *The Faerie Queene,* in which the raven is portrayed as dark and ominous:

> And over them sad Horrour with grim hew,
> Did always sore, beating his yron wings;
> And after him Owles and Night-ravens flew,
> The hateful messengers of heavy things,
> Of death and dolour telling sad tidings.

The raven appears not only as a messenger but also as a creature of the afterlife. This theme is evident in Cervantes's *Don Quixote,* written in the early 1600s:

> Have not your worships read the annals and
> histories of England, in which are recorded the
> famous deeds of King Arthur...with regard to
> whom it is an ancient tradition, and commonly
> received all over that kingdom of Great Britain,
> that this king did not die, but was changed by
> magic art into a raven, and that in process of
> time he is to return to reign and recover his
> kingdom and sceptre; for which reason it
> cannot be proved that from that time to this
> any Englishman ever killed a raven?

—FROM *DON QUIXOTE,*
MIGUEL DE CERVANTES SAAVEDRA, TRANSLATION BY JOHN ORMSBY, 1906

RAVEN

you

you   strut   you

caw you   clack

you clunk

like some brok-

en met-

al

thing   you

king   you   prince

of

great black birds

mag-

pie   jay   grackle

crow you   kaw you

slant

your

eye

at   me

darkbead   you

shrug

that

great

dark

wing

you

rau-   cous

cackle   laugh-

ing   shaggy-

throat-

ed   terror

you

—Sharon Brogan, 1988

The raven in this case is able to perform magic and to change shapes.

Other writers found the raven to be such a cunning creature that it deserved more than a mere reference within their works. Author Charles Dickens included a complex character named Grip, a devil raven, in *Barnaby Rudge*, his historical novel about the anti-Catholic riots of 1780.

> The raven, with his head very much on one side, and his bright eye shining like a diamond…replied in a voice so hoarse and distant, that it seemed to come through his thick feathers rather than out of his mouth.
>
> "Halloa, halloa, halloa! What's the matter here! Keep up your spirits. Never say die. Bow wow wow. I'm a devil, I'm a devil, I'm a devil. Hurrah!"…
>
> He…went to Barnaby—not in a hop, or walk, or run, but in a pace like that of a very particular gentleman with exceedingly tight boots on, trying to walk fast over loose pebbles. Then, stepping onto his extended hand, and condescending to be held out at arm's length, he gave vent to a succession of sounds, not unlike the drawing of some eight or ten dozen of long corks, and again asserted his brimstone birth and parentage with great distinctness.

Apparently Dickens was particularly fond of ravens, enjoying their comic antics, and he kept several as pets. He pays tribute to these pets in the 1868 preface to *Barnaby Rudge* (first published in

1841): "The raven in this story is a compound of two great originals, of whom I was, at different times, the proud possessor." Dickens described one of his birds as sleeping in the stable on top of a horse and routinely pirating the stable dog's dinner—fitting behavior for these thieving opportunists. Some believe that Dickens's Grip was the inspiration for Edgar Allan Poe's poem "The Raven."

The characters found in many pieces of literature reference the complexity of this versatile bird, while timeless fairy tales provide moral perspectives. Two tales about ravens—"The Raven" and "The Seven Ravens"—are included in *Grimm's Fairy Tales*. In "The Seven Ravens," a man and his wife have seven sons but long for a daughter. Their wishes are finally granted, but she is born small and sickly. The father sends his sons to the well to fetch some water to baptize his daughter. As they scramble to see who can get there first, the water pitcher falls into the depths of the well. When the sons do not return the father grows angry, fearing that his daughter might die without being baptized. He curses his sons, stating that he hopes they turn into ravens. Suddenly he hears a noise overhead and seven ravens fly off.

The daughter grows stronger and more comely, never knowing that she has any siblings. One day she overhears some people talking about her brothers, saying that it was her fault that they had been turned into ravens and had flown away. She feels compelled to rescue them. So she sets off with some bread and water and with a ring, which reminds her of her parents. The morning star tells her that her brothers may be found in the "glass mountain," so there she goes. A dwarf tells her that the ravens are not at home and invites her to wait for them. The dwarf goes about preparing meals for the ravens, and the sister eats a tiny bit from each of the seven plates and takes a sip from each of the seven drinking cups. In the last cup she places the ring she brought from home.

Upon returning to the glass mountain, the ravens immediately begin to eat. When the seventh brother gets to the bottom of his drinking cup, he discovers the ring and of course recognizes it. He hopes it is a sign that his sister is nearby and will rescue them. The sister runs to them, the ravens turn back into humans, and much kissing and hugging ensues.

"The Raven" has a similar story line. A naughty child is cursed by her queen mother, turns into a raven, and flies away. A man comes upon the raven in the forest and she asks for his help, informing him that she is actually the daughter of a king. She tells him to go to an old woman's house deep in the forest and wait for her. She warns him not to accept any food or drink from the woman or he will fall asleep and miss her. However, the man is persuaded by the old woman to eat and drink, after which he falls asleep. The raven princess comes by each day, but the man is always asleep. Finally she leaves him a note and a gold ring inscribed with her name. The note says to seek her out on the glass mountain. After a series of trials and tribulations that go on for a year or more, the man reaches her on the glass mountain, presents her with the ring, the curse is lifted, and they decide to get married the very next day.

In Hans Christian Andersen's "The Snow Queen," a raven helps little Gerda search for her lost playmate Kay. "Listen to me," says the raven to Gerda, "it is difficult to speak your language." The raven asks Gerda if she is able to understand Ravenish because it will be easier for them to communicate. "No, I have not learnt it," says Gerda, "but my grandmother understands it and she can speak gibberish too. I wish I had learnt it." Gerda recognizes the raven as wise and wishes she could understand Ravenish in order to learn from the all-knowing one.

In the 1867 story "Hans Huckebein" by German writer Wilhelm Busch, a youngster named Fritz decides he wants a pet raven. He proceeds to capture one and brings it home. The mischievous bird gets into all kinds of trouble around the house, pilfering food, disturbing clothing, and generally creating chaos. The raven then discovers a stash of alcohol, becomes inebriated, and entangles itself in some needlework. Unable to escape, it falls and hangs itself. The moral of the story: There are consequences for being naughty, and the clever and mischievous get themselves into trouble.

Ravens continue to be evident in modern literary culture, from ravishing raven-haired heroines in romance novels to contemporary plays, poetry, fiction, and screenplays. From the earliest publications known to man to those yet to be set forth, this bird with its multifaceted personality seems destined to continue influencing cultures everywhere.

Ravens and Crows in Art

Through the clear and rarefied atmosphere, the
Raven spreads his glossy wings and tail, and, as
he onward sails, rises higher and higher each bold
sweep that he makes, as if conscious that the
nearer he approaches the sun, the more splendent
will become the tints of his plumage.

—FROM *THE BIRDS OF AMERICA,*
JOHN JAMES AUDUBON, 1840

THROUGHOUT TIME, ravens and crows have inspired artists in all
parts of the world. Depictions of ravens appear in caves in Spain
and France, apparently drawn by Paleolithic peoples some 15,000
to 30,000 years ago. Even then they were associated with death;

many of the birds in these drawings are shown sitting on posts around burial sites.

In ancient Greek art, there are various paintings showing Apollo with his sacred bird, the raven, which served as both servant and messenger. In one Apollo sits on a stool strumming a lyre with one hand while holding a bowl in the other. He is wearing a crown of laurel leaves and is attended by a black raven. A French depiction of Apollo dating from 1410 likewise shows the sun god with a raven watching over him, but in this case the bird is white.

A piece of art from the Celtic era may still be seen at a Dunaverney bog in Antrim, Ireland. Here ravens are incorporated into a utilitarian object, a bronze flesh-hook. This was a tool used for moving and suspending pieces of meat for cooking. Two identical, three-dimensional raven silhouettes lie under the rings where the meat was hung. The ravens undoubtedly represented good luck in hunting.

John James Audubon, one of the finest nature artists in history, painted crows and ravens for his series *The Birds of America*. From the First Octavo Edition of this seven-volume text, Audubon offers admiration for this misunderstood bird:

> Notwithstanding the care of the Raven, his nest
> is invaded wherever it is found. His usefulness
> is forgotten, his faults are remembered and
> multiplied by imagination; and whenever he
> presents himself he is shot at, because from
> time immemorial ignorance, prejudice and
> destructiveness have operated on the mind of

man to his detriment... Some say they destroy
the Raven because he is black; others, because
his croaking is unpleasant and ominous! ... For
my part, I admire the Raven, because I see
much in him calculated to excite our wonder.

In Audubon's 1829 painting of the Common Raven, the bird
is sitting on the branch of a shellbark hickory tree (*Carya lacin-
iosa*), with mouth agape, loquacious as always. The carefully
painted blue on the feathers hints at the bird's iridescence.

It was in 1875 that the famous impressionist Édouard Manet
was asked to create five lithograph drawings for Stéphane
Mallarmé's French translation of Edgar Allan Poe's poem *The
Raven*. The two artists were living in Paris at the time.

In 1893, American artist Winslow Homer painted *The Fox
Hunt*. It depicts a pair of crows harassing a red fox on a field of snow.
The birds are presumably harbingers of death: the fox's life is close to
an end. Additional crows in the sky beyond add to the feeling of
doom.

Paul Gauguin's painting *Nevermore* (1897) shows a naked Poly-
nesian woman reclining on a bed, while an all-black bird, obviously a crow or raven, sits on the windowsill. The image of the
bird, along with the title of the painting, alludes to the Poe poem.

One of Vincent Van Gogh's last paintings in 1890 was of a
wheat field with crows. The eccentric, troubled artist reportedly
borrowed a gun to scare off the crows while he was painting, pur-
portedly to capture their essence in flight. The painting shows the

black birds flying in a starless sky and three paths through the wheat that lead to nowhere. Shortly after finishing this painting, Van Gogh used the gun to commit suicide. Some say the crows in his painting symbolize the inevitability of his death.

Edgar Allan Poe was not the only artist to become obsessed with ravens. Masahisa Fukase is a famous Japanese photographer who was once known for the cheerful pictures he took of his dearly beloved wife. After the marriage ended in 1976, the despondent Fukase became fascinated with the gloomy dark birds of death that were native to his Hokkaido homeland. He spent the next ten years photographing these birds, which was the basis for his book *The Solitude of Ravens.* The ravens often appear strong and elegant in his photos, and some think the birds resemble calligraphic markings. First published in Japan in 1986, *The Solitude of Ravens* was reprinted in the United States in 1991. Shortly thereafter, Fukase sustained a fall after an evening of drinking, and sadly, has been in a coma ever since.

Japanese painter Kawanabé Kyosai (1831–1899) was a master of Chinese ink and brush painting, and his work includes some excellent bird portrayals, including panel paintings of crows and ravens. Another renowned Japanese artist is Iwao Akiyama, who creates handsome woodblock prints of both species.

In 1999 Nobuo Kubota, a Vancouver-born artist with Japanese heritage, created a sculpture that he called *Mute Raven.* Made from wood, Styrofoam, canvas, and aluminum, this piece was the second in a series called *Homage to Birds, Beasts and Bugs.* Apparently Kubota began the piece as a protest statement about the destruction of wildlife, but it evolved into a symbol of silence. The raven is portrayed with bill closed, and, for the artist, serves as an instrument for calming the spirit.

The real stronghold of raven art has always been the Pacific Northwest coast. Here the raven has been the subject of wood carvings, elaborately crafted masks, and sculpted wooden pillars, known as totem poles.

Totem poles undoubtedly existed before the arrival of Europeans. Early poles were made from single pieces of cedar up to forty feet high, and they had distinctive forms and designs. Imagery used on the poles included creatures from the natural world such as eagles, whales, and ravens; humans; elements of nature such as the weather, the sun or the moon; and the supernatural. Since ravens were said to belong to both the natural and the spiritual worlds, they were the perfect inspiration for indigenous artists, and raven renderings abound. Totem poles were often enlivened by paint in shades of red, white, blue-green, and black. Interest in this art form continues to this day among both collectors and artists, and skillfully handcarved totem poles, both tall and short, command a high price—at least $500 per foot.

A totem is a symbol adopted by a Native American family or clan, and each clan uses a different animal as its totem. Many natural and spiritual beings were used. An eagle or raven crest served as a reminder of events that had occurred in the history of a particular clan. Intricately carved portal poles with identifying personalized crests were placed in front of houses to identify different clans' homes. The display of crests on poles, masks, and other regalia at public ceremonies confirmed ownership of them, designated the territory in which the crests were valid, and brought the strengths and powers associated with the crest to life. The raven has always been a particularly powerful totem because of its multifaceted personality and many different attributes: a seeker, a gatherer of information, a mischief maker that brings laughter and joy, a contradiction because it is both black and white, a helpful nurturing spirit, a shape-changer.

Totem poles were also created for storytelling purposes. Some of the stories were about the families or chiefs who requested the carving of the pole. Other poles reflected tales and legends, often about animals that were said to do important things, such as the raven. Pole stories were passed down from generation to generation, so that they would be remembered for all time.

Artists of the Haida tribe of the Queen Charlotte Islands traditionally sculpted miniature totems using argillite, a distinctive soft dark slate—the perfect medium for the glistening black raven. Wood carvings are another form of traditional Northwest Coast art. Renderings generally depict animals that are important to a particular culture, such as eagles, salmon, whales, bears—and ravens.

Masks are important in many aboriginal tribal cultures around the world, and some of the most striking and colorful have been those created by artists of the Pacific Northwest. Although masks were originally designed for use in ceremonies and rituals, mask-making has evolved into a contemporary art form.

The masks of the Pacific Northwest depicted many different animals and humans, including mythical creatures. Animal masks had special meaning for certain clans, since members of a tribe were said to be descended from specific animals. Narrative masks had stories or songs associated with them that documented historical and personal events, and they were passed down through families. Elaborate forehead masks worn by clan heads at various ceremonies and dance dramas are said to bring the supernatural to life. Feasts and rituals known as potlatches (potlatch means "to give," both of oneself as well as gifts) were meetings of chiefs and high-ranking people of a tribe who came together to witness certain claims: the rank of chief, territorial and property rights, name crests, marriage, inheritance, and death. These rituals could last several days to a month, although modern-day potlatches generally last only an evening.

Skillfully carved fetishes have been a notable art form in other Native American cultures. A fetish is an object, natural or manmade, in which a spirit is said to reside. They are believed to offer good fortune and protection, as well as hunting guidance from the carved animal, and ravens continue to be popular subjects. Carved from a variety of stones, fetishes are usually animals, and accordingly endowed with unique spiritual powers. Raven fetishes are often carved from black marble or jet, a dense black coal. Each fetish brings positive power in addition to having aesthetic appeal. Some say the raven fetish represents the power of healing. Others believe that the raven fetish helps us work through our shortcomings by reminding us that we have the power to transform anything we face.

Kachina dolls crafted by Hopi, and sometimes Navajo, artists may honor crows and ravens as well. Kachinas are thought to relate the spiritual world to the world of man. There are hundreds of different Kachinas, each with its own separate set of attributes, and each year Kachina spirits come and walk upon the earth, performing dances to bring about life and renewal. Kachina spirits come and go, and they sometimes pass over villages to bring rain. Ravens and crows also come and go, and since these birds share humans' food, their comings and goings are related to the presence and/or absence of rain clouds. In fact, the Crow Mother Kachina, with large crow wings on either side of the head, is thought to be the mother of all Kachinas and hence very powerful.

Ravens and crows have clearly been popular subjects with artists from a myriad of civilizations worldwide. Whether they are portrayed in battle banners or flags, sculpture, jewelry, woodcuts, fine paintings, etchings, t-shirts, decals, or tattoos, their influence on the artist community continues to be dramatic and inspiring.

Raven Lore

The Raven in Alaska was no ordinary bird.
He could change from a bird into a man and
could not only fly and walk, but could swim
underwater as fast as any fish.

—FROM AN ESKIMO LEGEND

THROUGHOUT HUMAN HISTORY, storytelling has served as a way for people to convey the fundamentals of day-to-day living, to pass along history and tradition, and, of course, to entertain. Few animals have received as much attention in legend and lore as the raven: there is a tale to represent each and every one of the bird's characteristics. Taken together, these narratives indicate a general ambivalence toward these paradoxical birds with their multifarious personalities. Although the tales are somewhat contradictory from culture to culture, one thing is sure: the sheer number of stories is indicative of the importance of ravens throughout history.

Reverence for ravens reached its highest level among the early peoples of the Pacific Northwest, where the bird was believed to have created the world, or at least some very important components of it. The raven brought light to an otherwise dark world by releasing the sun, moon, and stars; it discovered man; and it

The Raven and the First Men by Bill Reid (Haida), 1980.

ensured that the ocean tides would continue to ebb and flow. Here's how the stories go:

A Haida legend tells of human beings materializing out of a giant clamshell that was discovered by a raven on a strip of sand. The clamshell was full of tiny creatures, all of which were cowering in terror in the presence of the black-cloaked raven. The bird coaxed and coerced the little creatures to come out by telling them of the great red cedar trees that they could use to build houses, canoes, and totem poles; it told of the salmon in the rivers and the whales, sea lions, porpoises, and many other fish that would feed them forever. Mainly the raven wanted the tiny creatures to come out of the clamshell so that it could have someone to play with, because it was bored. Finally, after much wheedling the tiny creatures emerged, and the raven amused himself with these new playthings for quite a while, in the process teaching them many things. Later on, the conniving bird changed the rivers so that they flowed in one direction only, making it difficult for humans to travel.

An Unalit or Yup'ik Eskimo story about the first human differs from the clamshell story in that it claims man emerged from a plant. The first man lay coiled up in the pod of a beach-pea plant. After four days in the seed pod, he stretched out his legs and feet and burst out. He fell to the ground and then stood up as a full-grown man. He naturally surveyed his surroundings and suddenly noticed a dark object flying in his direction. It was a raven. The bird stopped, raised a wing, pushed up its bill to the top of its head as if it were a mask, and transformed into a man. The raven-man asked the pea-pod escapee who he was and where he was from. The pea-pod man answered that he had emerged from the pea pod and pointed to the plant. "Ah," exclaimed the raven, "I made that vine but didn't realize that anything quite like you would ever come from it!"

Several cultures attribute the creation of light to the raven. In the ancient mythology of east China, ravens were considered symbols of the sun, and the solar symbol of ancient China was the raven encompassed in a circle. In the mythology of Japan, Yatagarasu is the raven that belongs to Amaterasu, the sun goddess, and in Korean mythology, the raven is known as Samjogo. From the Pacific Northwest comes the following saga about how the raven stole the sun and illuminated the earth:

Long ago the world was in complete darkness. Tired and frustrated and somewhat bored with having to fumble around in the pitch-black, the raven decided to do something about this state of affairs. He knew, in his all-knowing, sagacious way, that a certain family had stolen and hidden the sun. So he decided he would rescue it, using his magical powers. He transformed himself into an infant. The family saw the baby and thought it was so cute that they brought it home to their lodge. The raven decided he would annoy the family by continually crying and screaming. As the family wondered what the baby wanted, with all of this carrying on, the disguised raven pointed to a carved cedar box, a bentwood box, in the corner of the room. So the family gave him the box so that he would stop screaming. When no one was watching, the raven transformed himself back into a bird and, with a loud *croak,* picked up the box and flew out through the lodge's smoke hole. As the raven flew, he opened the box containing the sun, and sunlight flooded the world. (Bentwood boxes are medium-sized and made from one piece of wood, generally cedar, steamed and bent, and are functional as well as decorative for peoples of the Northwest coast.)

There are other versions of the light story. In Inuit folklore, the raven is thought to have created light after it cast glittering bits of mica across the skies. The Milky Way is the result. Other renditions claim that the raven stole a ball of light from an old man's box and ferried it away but then dropped it after being chased by an eagle. The sphere broke into pieces, one quite large and many other tiny shards. The miniscule bits of light bounced back into the sky and became the stars; the other half of the sphere formed the sun and the moon.

Another adaptation, by Tlingit artist and photographer Larry McNeil (whose work often includes ravens), tells the story this way: In the beginning a powerful chief possessed the moon and the sun, keeping them tucked away in boxes in his home. The raven was getting pretty tired of having to conduct his business in complete darkness, so the disgruntled bird flew to the chief's house to assess the situation. The chief had a daughter, and every day she would ramble down to a nearby stream to fetch water. The raven followed and changed itself into the needle of a spruce tree, which floated down the watercourse and was caught in the daughter's water receptacle. After the needle was in the water, the daughter took a drink, and she became pregnant by the raven/spruce needle. A healthy baby boy was the result. The chief loved his new grandson and lavished attention on him, but there was one thing he would not let him do: he was not to touch the boxes containing the sun and the moon. One day the baby/raven decided to throw the tantrum of all tantrums until his grandfather agreed to let him play with the boxes that contained the light. The baby/raven quickly snatched the sun and escaped through the house's smoke hole, turning black in the process. With a toss of its bill the raven released the sun into the sky.

The raven was also said to be responsible for oceanic tides, according to Tlingit lore. When the world was new, the raven and his people lived near the shore of the Big Water, but at that time there were no tides and the people could get food only from creatures that washed up on the shore. The people were unable to go out into the Big Water to hunt for tasty morsels because the water was too deep. The raven realized that soon there wouldn't be sufficient food to fill his own hungry belly. So he sat down to ponder the problem, fell asleep, and dreamed that the Great Spirit told him of a cave at the end of the world, and of a woman who lived there. This woman held the tide line, which controlled the rising and falling of the Big Water. The Great Spirit suggested to the raven that if he could persuade her to let go of the line, the water would recede and good things to eat would be uncovered.

The raven awoke from his dream and flew by day and by night until he came to the cave and saw the old woman holding the tide line. He diverted her attention by rubbing his belly and carrying on about the delicious clams he had just eaten. While the woman was distracted, the raven was able to move in and kick sand into her eyes. As she tried to brush the sand out of her eyes, she accidentally released the tide line; the water fell back, and soon some of the beach was uncovered. The raven flew home, thinking of all the delectable items he would soon be feasting upon.

For many days, the raven and his people ate the nutritious and tasty foods uncovered from the Big Water. Soon, however, many of the creatures that were providing food for the raven and his people began to die. The people turned to the clever raven for assistance, and the bird decided to return to the cave. The woman was still trying to get the sand out of her eyes, but she heard the raven approach. "You tricked me!" she cried. The raven then told her about all the creatures that were dying because the Big Water that was their home no longer covered them, and about how little the people had to eat. The raven said he would help her get the sand out of her eyes if she would be willing to let go of the tide line from time to time, so that the people would be able to harvest some of the good food from the Big Water. The woman agreed, and that is how the tides began.

Many indigenous peoples believed the raven to be a prominent supernatural being that could rapidly change its appearance or form. Like a chameleon, the raven would appear in different places in different guises—as an animal, bird, or human. Because of its inherent sense of mischief, it sometimes changed form simply to entertain itself. At other times its motives were seemingly more virtuous, and it would alter the circumstances of a particular village, hopefully for the better.

In a tale from the Salish tribe of Vancouver Island, the less desirable characteristics of the raven are noted: One crisp fall day, the raven and his little sisters, who were crows, decided they would go on a blackberry-picking expedition. In his all-knowing way, the raven said he knew just where to go to find lots of ripe, juicy fruits—and it was only a short canoe-ride away. The birds gathered up their baskets and got into the canoe. The raven said he would paddle first, but he grew tired quickly; he felt very sleepy and thought a nap would be an excellent idea. He promised the crows that he would help them pick berries once they reached their location, if he could only sleep for a while.

When the canoe landed at their destination, the raven awoke with a start. He pointed in the direction of the blackberry plants and said that he would, of course, help them unload their baskets into the canoe, but he was still very tired and sleepy. The crows went into the woods, and the raven went to sleep, awakening only when the crows returned to the canoe with loads of fruit. After delivering this first batch, the crows returned to the berry brambles to collect more of the succulent fruits. And the raven began to eat the fruit. This went on all day long—the crows picking and delivering the berries to the canoe, and the raven eating the fruits of their harvest.

By the end of day, the raven became cognizant of the fact that he had eaten nearly all the blackberries. Realizing that the crows might be unhappy, to put it mildly, the raven decided to make up a story regarding how the berries had disappeared. First he removed some of his tail feathers and threw them into the water, casting a spell upon them (an easy feat for this transforming trickster) so that they resembled enemy war canoes. The raven then noticed that his chest was quite stained from the juice of all the berries he had consumed. So he carefully plucked a few feathers from his breast so that he would look mussed up and bedraggled. Finally, he scattered about the very few remaining berries and the baskets, and pretended to collapse on the beach.

When the crows returned, the raven began to moan and carry on. Enemy raiders had attacked, he said, and he was unable to fight them off; they had stolen all of the berries. To show that a struggle had taken place, he pointed to his bloody chest. The raven also told the crows that if they looked out to sea, they could still see the war canoes. The trusting crows believed the raven and felt bad that he had been wounded. Secretly, the raven smiled because he was certain that his deception had been successful.

As the raven and crows were preparing to leave to return home, a small snail appeared and called out. The snail proclaimed that he had seen everything that went on, that there had been no raid by the enemy, and that the lazy and greedy raven had devoured all the berries that the crows had picked. The raven denied these accusations, of course, stating that the snail was lying. The crows grew angry, but the raven told them to look out to sea, for the enemy canoes were still in sight. Unfortunately for the raven, the spell on his tail feathers had worn off, and the crows noticed that the "enemy canoes" were only feathers. Then they realized that the blood on the raven's chest was not blood at all, but rather berry juice. The furious crows began to mob the raven and insisted that he paddle the canoe the entire way back to the village. There they put him on the spot, so that he had to explain to everyone why there would be no blackberries for dinner that night.

From the Northwest Territories comes another raven trickster tale: After a hunter discovered a run of seal breathing-holes in the ice, he decided to search for a camping place. A raven appeared and pointed out an area located beneath a mountain, telling the man that it was where all hunters camped. So the man elected to camp there. During the night a large boulder rolled down the mountain and crushed the man to death. As the raven pecked out the dead man's eyes, he said to himself, "Why do all these hunters believe my silly tales?"

The Cherokee believed in some frightful evil beings known as the Kalanu Ahyeli-ski, or raven mockers. Raven mockers were said to kill their victims, then cut out their hearts and eat them. Raven mockers were invisible and their cuts left no scars. However, there was medicine to use against these wicked creatures, and the Cherokee relied upon good medicine people to maintain vigils at the bedsides of sick persons. As long as the doctors were present, the raven mockers were afraid to approach. If illness claimed the life of a victim, the medicine man stayed with the body until burial. Once the body was placed underground, the raven mockers could not steal the heart. These ghastly creatures appear in the following tale:

One day a man was out hunting and realized that darkness was falling. He sought shelter at a nearby house. No one was home, so he decided to lie down in a corner of the room, where he promptly fell asleep. Suddenly he heard the cry of a raven, and then the old man who owned the house came in and sat down by the fire. A second raven called out, and the old man's wife entered. The young man grew frightened, for he knew immediately that they were raven mockers. He kept quiet and stayed hidden in the dark corner of the house. The man asked his wife about her hunting success that day, and she replied that she had not been lucky because there were too many doctors watching. The man said he was more fortunate and brought forth some meat for the wife to cook. The piece of meat looked just like a human heart.

While the meat was cooking on the roasting spit, the wife kept hearing strange noises—they almost sounded like snoring—and she insisted that they were not alone. The old man argued back that she was just hearing things. This argument went back and forth several times. Suddenly the fire blazed brightly and the room lit up. The old man spotted the mysterious sleeper and shook him awake. By this time it was morning, and the woman left the room to go fix breakfast. As she prepared the meal she began to sob and cry. The old man explained to the hunter that his wife was sorrowful because she had recently lost some of her friends. But the hunter knew the real reason for her crying: she was frightened that she had been discovered for who she really was—a witch.

When the meal was ready, the hunter ate a bowl of corn mush. The old man apologized for the fact that they did not have any meat, saying that they hadn't had any for a long, long time. After finishing off his mush meal, the hunter departed. The old man ran after him and gave him some exquisite wampum beadwork, asking the hunter not to mention that he and his wife had argued. The hunter accepted the beads but later threw them into a nearby stream and returned to his home village. There he told everyone about the entire experience. Realizing that they were up against raven mockers, a village war party gathered and returned to destroy the old man and his wife. But when they arrived they found the couple lying dead in the house. So the war party set the house on fire and burned the two witches together.

In contrast to the raven's naughty and wicked behavior noted in the Salish and Cherokee tales, in an Aleut fable from southwest Alaska a raven meets a princess, and their meeting results in a favorable outcome: A certain Aleut chief really did not care for the raven because that shape-changing bird could transform itself into almost anything it felt like. The chief had a lovely princess daughter, and when the raven saw her he thought about turning himself into a human. But knowing of the chief's disdain for him, the raven had another idea. He told the princess that he was going to fly above the river and turn himself into a hemlock needle. The needle would float down the river and when she saw it, she should pick it up and swallow it. The princess nodded in agreement, but wondered what all of this meant. What was really going to happen?

The raven flew off into the sky and suddenly a hemlock needle drifted down towards the water. When it reached the princess, she did as the raven had told her. She picked it up and swallowed it. At first she was puzzled because nothing seemed to be happening. After a few minutes, however, she felt a sharp jerking sensation in her back. When she reached around to see what was happening, she discovered that she had sprouted feathers. A wing had grown out of her back and wrapped itself around her, making her feel warm and loved. The raven and the princess were joined together forever. Every creature they encountered could sense the love that emanated from the face of the princess and from the wing of the raven.

People of the Pueblo tribes of New Mexico thought that the comings and goings of the dark birds signified the presence or absence of black clouds. Crows and ravens could be counted upon to arrive with the black rain clouds of summer. Rain—as well as corn—could be stolen, causing drought, sickness, and evil. At harvest time ravens and crows would stop in to eat corn and as a result many associated them with agriculture.

The Zunis tell a tale about the origin of the raven and the macaw, a large colorful parrot with a long tail: A priest named Yanauluha carried a plumed staff covered with many colorful feathers. Shells were attached to the staff and made a pleasing tinkling sound. When people saw the priest with his staff, they asked many questions. So the priest struck the staff on a hard surface and blew upon the feathers, and within the plumes there appeared four eggs. Two were sky blue and two were an earthy dun-red color.

The priest told the people that the eggs were the seeds of living beings and asked them to choose which they would follow. From two of the eggs would come beings with beautifully colored feathers. Wherever they flew it would always be summer, and an abundance of crops would flourish without effort. The other two eggs would produce evil creatures, spotted with black and white. Wherever they flew it would always be winter and the fields would produce crops only with much toil and labor.

The priest asked the people which they would choose. The people who were strongest chose the blue eggs. They put the eggs in soft sand on the sunny side of a hill and watched them day after day. When they finally hatched, the emerging pin feathers showed colors of yellow, blue, red, and green, so the people thought they had the macaws, and food and summer weather were assured. They fed the young birds all kinds of foods that they themselves enjoyed, thus teaching the birds to eat all desirable food. But when the young birds' feathers grew in, they were black with white bandings. They were ravens, who proceeded to fly away laughing and croaking.

The other two eggs—the dull ones—became colorful macaws and by the toss of the priest's wand were carried to the land of summer far, far away. Those who chose the raven became the Raven People; they were winter people and were very strong. Those who chose the macaw became the Macaw People, or summer people. The Macaw People were fewer in number and less strong, but they were considered wiser because they were more deliberate.

In Hopi country of the American Southwest, American crows are more widely distributed than ravens, but they also are respected by the Hopis for their sagacity and other human qualities. However, the Hopis also express some ambivalence about these birds. Ravens and crows eat beans and corn, two kinds of foods eaten by humans. Because the birds also eat dead things, the Hopis find them repugnant. There are separate Hopi words for the two species: crow is *angwusi* and raven is *adoko*.

There is a Hopi fable about a youngster trapped on a precipitous cliff face who is saved by a raven. The strong-flying bird flaps its way to the rocky cliff and tells the frightened lad to climb aboard. With the boy safely settled on his mighty back, Adoko flies directly back to the boy's home village, and he is saved. Because of this story, Adoko is often referred to as Raven the Rescuer.

Nearly every raven characteristic is embodied in tales from a multitude of cultures throughout the world. Many of these stories credit the raven for the existence of some basic elements of our world—the sun, the moon, the stars, and the tides. Many of these myths also allude to the attributes of love and guidance as well as hurt and betrayal. As you can probably surmise from these many tales, few creatures have enjoyed so much attention and reverence as the—anything but common—raven.

Conservation Status in North America

Make prayers to the Raven.
Raven that is,
Raven that was,
Raven that always will be.
Make prayers to the Raven.
Raven, bring us luck.

—PRAYER OF THE KOYUKON,
NATIVE PEOPLE OF ALASKA

THE CORVID FAMILY has inhabited North America since pre-historic times. Fossils indicate that crows have been on the continent for a long, long time—probably some two million years—and it is likely that ravens preceded their smaller cousins in arriving here from Asia. With their larger size and stronger capabilities for flying, ravens were more suited for traveling across isthmuses or narrow strips of terra firma that connected larger masses of land. Wolves and their early ancestors also journeyed across land bridges and may have been a factor in the advance of ravens, because they provided feeding opportunities for the birds. Likewise, hunter-gatherers from Siberia crossed the Bering Strait to what is now known as Alaska thousands of years ago, and were probably kept company by these scavenging black birds as well. Fossil remains of ravens have been discovered in some of the earliest known camping grounds in areas of western Canada, pointing to an association between the birds and the people of North America for more than 10,000 years.

Ravens have always utilized human beings and other animals as valuable resources. This behavior is something ornithologists call autolycism. Essentially it means taking advantage of and using opportunities that are provided by the activities of other animals, including humans. For example, many birds use the skins of reptiles or pieces of human-manufactured cloth for nesting materials. Crows are known to pluck mammal hair for lining their nests. Ravens sometimes nest on man-made billboards or under highway overpasses. Both also dine on animal carcasses killed by wolves or by automobiles. Corvids may also be found in fields, striding about, near the feet of cattle or other range animals in order to eat insects stirred up by the movement of the grazers.

It wasn't until the early twentieth century that raven populations took a dive in many areas of North America, and they disappeared

Ravens and Crows of North America

It's relatively easy to see ravens and crows in North America. Wherever there is a supply of food, a crow or raven may be nearby. The corvid species found in North America are listed in taxonomic order with their ranges and habitats noted.

American Crow, *Corvus brachyrhynchos*
RANGE & HABITAT: throughout most of North America except in hottest desert regions; open country, farmlands, suburbs, beaches, and open woods
LENGTH: 17.5"
WINGSPAN: 39"
VOICE: harsh *caw caw*
STATUS: range expanding

Northwestern Crow, *Corvus caurinus*
RANGE & HABITAT: northwest coast, southern Alaska to Olympic Peninsula in Washington; coastal coniferous forests, along beaches and shoreline
LENGTH: 16"
WINGSPAN: 34"
VOICE: *caw* is lower and hoarser than American Crow's
STATUS: may be hybridizing with American Crow

Tamaulipas Crow, *Corvus imparatus*
RANGE & HABITAT: northeastern Mexico; uncommon winter visitor to southernmost Texas, where it frequents landfills
LENGTH: 14.5"
WINGSPAN: 30"
VOICE: low froglike *croak*
STATUS: probably stable

Fish Crow, *Corvus ossifragus*
RANGE & HABITAT: eastern U.S. coast, southeastern U.S. through Florida, west along rivers to Oklahoma and Texas; usually near water—coast and inland along rivers, salt marshes, tidal flats
LENGTH: 15.5"
WINGSPAN: 36"
VOICE: high, nasal *kah hah*
STATUS: range expanding

Common Raven, *Corvus corax*
RANGE & HABITAT: common in the North and West; forests, mountains, deserts, coastline
LENGTH: 24"
WINGSPAN: 53"
VOICE: deep, drawn-out *croak*
STATUS: scarce in the East, but increasing

from much of the eastern and midwestern regions. Their disappearance was blamed on a variety of factors, including poisons and baited traps, the demise of American bison and wolves (two mammals that were important to ravens for locating and providing food sources), deforestation, the conversion of more land to agriculture, and an increasing population of crows, which created a strain on available habitat and food resources. Nothing suggests that populations declined significantly in the North or in the West at that time.

Fortunately, raven numbers began to increase in the second half of the twentieth century. It was in the 1950s that ravens began inhabiting cities in the Saskatchewan province of Canada, searching for bits of refuse. Since the late 1960s populations have increased throughout much of North America, and by 1976 they had returned to the Northeast, learning to acclimate to more populated areas. In the Central Valley of California a staggering increase in numbers was reported between 1968 and 1992. Factors affecting populations undoubtedly vary from location to location. For example, in regions with extremely harsh winters, access to carcasses may be a limiting factor.

But in general these adaptable birds have survived relatively recent persecution and have been expanding their range, especially in the northeast region of North America. They are also spreading southward and reestablishing their populations in areas that they formerly occupied. In western North America today, they may be found in Alaska and Canada; the United States from the Pacific Coast east to Montana, east-central Wyoming, east-central Colorado, western Oklahoma, and Texas; and south into Mexico. In the eastern United States, they can be found in Minnesota, northern Michigan, the Canadian border south to New Hampshire, western Massachusetts, northwestern Connecticut, much of New York, northwestern New Jersey west through Pennsylvania, west Maryland, West Virginia, southeastern Kentucky, westernmost North Carolina, South Carolina, and northern Georgia.

THE STATUS OF THE COMMON RAVEN is variable throughout its habitat range, and estimating densities of the species is difficult. Many of the birds live in large groups that wander about and roost communally; others stay in mated pairs or by themselves. Ravens are protected by the Migratory Bird Treaty Act of 1918, which makes it unlawful to pursue, hunt, kill, or sell birds that are listed. Basically this act provides for the protection of some 800 species, not all of which are migratory. It should be noted, however, that ravens and crows were not actually placed on the list until 1972, and in some states crows are regarded as legal game birds.

Unlike crows, ravens continue to enjoy wide admiration and respect. The effects of human activity will certainly play a role in their future. In some areas, the birds are shy and sensitive to the presence of humans; in other situations they are abundant and considered bothersome. As long as they are associated with garbage many people will consider them to be pests. Some people advocate changing garbage disposal methods, either by burning garbage more regularly or by compacting and covering refuse with fill dirt. Dumpsters with self-closing lids might be another option for restaurants and businesses to discourage dumpster diving by ravens.

RAVENS CONTINUE TO INTRIGUE MANKIND, and it is likely that further studies will be done on these "bird brains." Researchers point to a need for further studies on the birds' morphology and geographical distribution in terms of genetic divergence. Investigations into the parasites and diseases affecting ravens are indicated, and their vocalizations continue to be rather mysterious.

Because of the Common Raven's supreme adaptivity, its marauding feeding habits, and its ability to benefit from the resources provided by human activities, it seems likely that its population will remain stable and possibly even increase. Given its widespread distribution worldwide, it seems likely that despite Edgar Allan Poe's repetitive refrain "nevermore," these birds will continue to flourish and exist "evermore."

Life Expectancy

In captivity, Common Ravens may live to the ripe old age of forty years or more. Larger birds tend to have a longer life expectancy than small birds. However, there are many hazards to birds in nature, and ravens rarely reach their second decade in the wild. Many birds are hit and killed by moving vehicles; others are electrocuted on power lines. Raven eggs and young are vulnerable to birds of prey, other ravens, and coyotes. Since ravens spend a fair amount of time on the ground, they are susceptible to poisons and traps. Apparently the West Nile virus is also of concern for these birds.

Suggested Resources and Additional Reading

American Society of Crows and Ravens (ASCAR), www.ascaronline.org, offers an overview of the raven's behavior and diet and related links.

Angell, Tony. *Ravens, Crows, Magpies, and Jays*. Seattle, WA: University of Washington Press, 1978.

Boarman, W. I., and B. Heinrich. "Common Raven (*Corvus corax*)." *The Birds of North America* No. 476. Ithaca, NY: Cornell Lab of Ornithology and the American Ornithologists' Union, 1999.

Feher-Elston, Catherine. *Ravensong: A Natural and Fabulous History of Ravens and Crows*. New York, NY: Jeremy P. Tarcher/Penguin, 2004.

Goodchild, Peter, ed. *Raven Tales*. Chicago, IL: Chicago Review Press, 1991.

Goodwin, Derek. *Crows of the World*. New York: Cornell University Press, 1976.

Heinrich, Bernd. *Mind of the Raven: Investigations and Adventures with Wolf-Birds*. New York: Cliff Street Books, 1999.

———. *Ravens in Winter*. New York: Vintage Books, 1989.

Kilham, Lawrence. *The American Crow and the Common Raven*. College Station, TX: Texas A&M University Press, 1989.

Marzluff, John M., and Angell, Tony M. *In the Company of Crows and Ravens*. Connecticut: Yale University Press, 2005.

Savage, Candace. *Bird Brains: The Intelligence of Crows, Ravens, Magpies, and Jays*. San Francisco, CA: Sierra Club, 1997.

Photo and Illustration Credits